WILLIAMSON
Little Hands ®

WOW! I'M READING!

Fun Activities
to
Make Reading Happen

JILL FRANKEL HAUSER

ILLUSTRATIONS BY STAN JASKIEL

WILLIAMSON PUBLISHING COMPANY · CHARLOTTE, VERMONT

Little Hands®, *Kids Can!*®, *Tales Alive!*® *and Kaleidoscope Kids*® are registered trademarks of Williamson Publishing Company. *Good Times*™ and *Quick Starts*™ *for Kids!*are trademarks of Williamson Publishing.

Library of Congress Cataloging-in-Publication Data
Hauser, Jill Frankel, 1950-
    Wow! I'm Reading!: fun activities to make reading happen / Jill Frankel Hauser.
        p. cm. — (A Williamson Little Hands book)
    Includes index.
    ISBN 1-885593-41-4
    1. Reading (early childhood) 2. Early childhood education—Activity programs. I.
Title. II. Series.

LB1139.5.R43 H39 2000
372.41'6—dc21

99-089816

Little Hands!® series editor: Susan Williamson
Design: Hopkins/Baumann
Design Management: Jennifer Dixon
Design Assistant: Nadira Vlaun
Illustrations: Stan Jaskiel
Cover Design: Trezzo-Braren Studio
Printing: Capital City Press

Williamson Publishing Co.
Box 185
Charlotte, VT 05445
(800) 234-8791

Manufactured in the United States of America

10 9 8 7 6 5 4 3 2 1

Notice: The information contained in this book is true, complete, and accurate to the best of our knowledge. All recommendations and usages are made without any guarantees on the part of the author or Williamson Publishing. The author and publisher disclaim all liability incurred in conjunction with the use of this information.

DEDICATION

TO LINDA FISHER, YOUR CONVICTION THAT KNOWLEDGE AND SKILLS EMPOWER YOUNG CHILDREN ALWAYS HAS BEEN AN INSPIRATION.

ACKNOWLEDGEMENT

MANY THANKS AND HUGS TO MY ROTHER SCHOOL KINDERGARTNERS FOR YOUR VORACIOUS APPETITE TO LEARN AND YOUR WILLINGNESS TO TRY ANYTHING! THANKS ALSO TO OUR PARSONS MIDDLE SCHOOL AND ENTERPRISE HIGH SCHOOL TEEN MENTORS. YOUR ENTHUSIASM AND COMPASSION MAKE US TRULY A COMMUNITY OF LEARNERS.

CONTENTS

TO BEGINNING

Becoming a reader is like growing up — it doesn't happen all at once. You hardly notice that you're learning, but you can tell you know so much more about letters and words than you did as a baby. Do you like listening to stories and looking at books? Can you read a stop sign or the name of your favorite store? Can you write some of the letters in your name? Then you already know a lot about how to read!

READERS

Come join in the fun of learning to read and write. Let's play with words and letters, rhymes, and tales. You'll be building the skills you need to become a super reader and writer. It won't be long before you'll be reading any book you like. You'll read directions to make and do things, and you'll write about whatever is on your mind. The world of terrific tales will be open to you anytime, anywhere!

TO GROWN-UPS

Young children are readers. Just think of how they love turning the pages and retelling tales from favorite storybooks. Young children are writers. Hand a child a pencil, and she'll promptly take your order for her make-believe restaurant.

The literacy activities in this book not only support a child's sense that she is already a reader, they give her the skills to truly become one! Some activities are language games that can easily be played on the go. These simple yet powerful ways to play with the sounds of language will make learning phonics easy and meaningful.

Because the alphabet is central to literacy, the activities in this book empower children with mastery of every aspect: letter recognition, formation, and sound.

Writing is an interactive way for young children to experience the dynamics of print. So the writing activities included here encourage all attempts, from those early scribbles to spelling and sounding out words. Best of all, we'll show you how to transform your home or classroom into a literacy-rich laboratory where print will have meaning. Here a child can explore the fascinating world of spoken and written language, stories, and ideas.

Learning to read requires many literacy experiences over time, so the activities are designed to be shared again and again. You'll find a main activity that introduces a key concept or skill. More Fun For You! invites

children to practice the same skill in new ways. Teaching Time offers valuable insights into the learning process and tells why the activity is effective.

All activities are adaptable to a wide range of abilities. Whether you model reading for a child or share in the process, or the child independently figures out the words on the page, everyone can join in the learning fun.

A Peek at the Process
What sort of knowledge do children need to become readers and writers? To find out, let's see what it takes to read and spell the word *cat.* For most kids, a cat is that warm, furry critter who cuddles on your lap and gives you a rough, wet kiss.

But to become successful readers and writers, kids must think of cat in a completely different way and learn lots of new concepts:
◆ Letters represent sounds. The letters **c, a,** and **t** each stand for a particular sound.

◆ Strung together, letters form words. The letters **c–a–t** = *cat.*
◆ To figure out the word, the sounds are uttered in order. The child holds onto each sound while moving to the next one, and **c a t** becomes *cat!*
◆ Words have meaning. Those blended-together sounds sound like a familiar word — cat!

So to read, a child has got to know what letters and words are. He must be able to match a particular sound to a particular letter symbol, then be able to blend those sounds together in the correct order. What he utters ought to sound familiar and make sense (like "cat").

Writing requires the same skills in reverse order. Let's give it a try:
◆ Words are separate units of meaning. The utterance "cat" is a word that refers to a favorite pet.
◆ Words contain separate sound units. *Cat* has three: **c a t.**
◆ Each sound is represented by a particular symbol, called a letter. The sound **c** is represented by **c.**
◆ To form words, letters are written in the same order that the sounds are uttered.

So to write, a child has got to know a word (like *cat*), be able to "unglue" that word into its separate sound parts **(c a t),** search his mind for the letter symbols that represent each of those sounds **(c, a, t),** and then, write those symbols down in the correct order *(cat).* At last!

And that's just what it takes to figure out a single word. Imagine reading or writing an entire sentence. The child also must understand the structure of spoken language: how words connect together to have meaning. No small task!

Now back to the part about the cuddly critter. Comprehension is based on experience. If someone has shared a book about cats with that child, she will already have a sense of what words and letters are all about. If she loved the book, she'll begin to understand the payoff for making the effort to read the word cat. And if reading *cat* successfully jogs her memory to recall one of life's rich experiences, reading becomes super fun and meaningful! Someday she'll have the power to make sense of the print around her, print that contains a wonderful world of stories and fantastic facts about her favorite furry friend!

PHONEMIC AWARENESS: WHAT'S IT ALL ABOUT?

Phonemic awareness — it's the mysterious-sounding buzzword that demystifies phonics for kids. Simply put, phonemic awareness is the understanding that spoken words consist of a sequence of sounds. Whether or not this understanding "clicks" can determine a child's level of success as a reader. Here's a sampling of activities that build phonemic awareness:

◆ Rhyming: Think of words that rhyme with *hot, dot, cot…*
◆ Counting syllables: How many syllables in the word *fish? candy? dinosaur?*
◆ Same-sound matching: Think of a word with the same beginning sound as *pie, pancake,* and *potato.*
◆ Blending sounds: Can you guess my slow-sounding word: **mmmaaannn**?
◆ Breaking words into sounds (segmentation): What three sounds do you hear in the word *book?* **b-oo-k**
◆ Sound manipulation: Take the **t** from trip. What word is left? Change the **a** in cat to **u**. What's the new word?

Because kids are exploring sounds in phonemic awareness (not symbols), no worksheets, pencils, or flash cards are needed. Kids can practice phonemic awareness through language play on the go, anytime, anywhere — and the more practice, the better!

To Sum Up:

1. Reading takes knowing about letters and words (print awareness).

2. It requires ear training (recognizing sounds in words) and eye training (recognizing letter symbols).

3. Link symbols to sounds (phonics), and a child can figure out most words written in our alphabetic code.

4. Those words only have meaning (comprehension) if they relate back to an experience the child has been given language to define and appreciate (concept and language development).

A Sound Start

Let's start with ear training because sound awareness is absolutely critical to reading success. As we saw in the *cat* example above, readers must be able to identify the individual sound units (phonemes) that make up words. Why? Because the code we use to record speech happens to be alphabetic — written symbols represent spoken sounds. So understanding phonemes, called phonemic awareness, is the key to figuring out that code. It's no surprise that a child's level of phonemic awareness is one of the most reliable predictors of reading achievement.

What makes building awareness of phonemes a challenge is that kids (and adults) are not used to listening for them. In fact, if we paid attention to the sounds of words instead of the sense of words, we'd never understand what people were saying! Yet to become readers and writers, kids must do just that: Listen to sounds and hear language in this new way.

From hearing words (units with meaning, like *banana*), to syllables (sound units like **ba-na-na**), to phonemes (the smallest sound units like **b a n a n a**), the child is trying to identify increasingly less meaningful units of speech, so the task becomes more and more difficult.

Building phonemic awareness does not happen overnight. And it's tough to learn because sound awareness is so abstract. The good news is that it's best developed through play — joyous experimentation with the sounds of language: songs with great rhythms and rhymes, fun language games, nursery rhyme classics, and Dr. Seuss-style books. Check out the Sound Start activities in Chapter 2 for fun with phonemes.

The Eyes Have It

All the phonemic awareness in the world won't make a child a reader unless that understanding is coupled with print awareness. As we saw in the *cat* example on page 8, readers must be able to identify letter symbols and link them to particular sounds. That's exactly how our alphabet works: The alphabet is a code of written symbols that represent spoken sounds. Recognizing letters and identifying sounds correctly are critical to figuring out that code, so they're both powerful predictors of reading ability.

To become capable readers, kids must focus on the abstract shapes and lines we call letters. There are 52 symbols, uppercase and lowercase, in hundreds of fonts (typefaces) that actually look quite similar to each other. To get an idea of the difficulty of this task, just take a look at text in the alphabet of a language you don't speak. That's how all letters look to a young child.

So how can we give kids ownership of the alphabet? Celebrate each marvelous letter though the vivid learning experiences described in Chapter 4. Point out print everywhere and all the time. From the letters in your child's name to the barrage of print she sees from her car seat, think of the world as a giant set of flash cards for learning!

Print Power

Kids are driven to explore and figure things out. Everything in their environment is up for discovery — including print. And it's a good thing because there's so much to learn about how print works: What's print for? What's a letter? A word? In which direction are words read? These questions and more are answered when kids grow up in a print-rich world with an informative grown-up as their guide.

While most kids can identify the McDonald's sign, it's those who are guided to look beyond the logo and focus on the letters who first catch on to what print is all about. Give kids extra oomph from a read-aloud story with on-the-spot literacy lessons: Point out the title of the book, how words are separated by spaces, and track each read-aloud word with your finger.

Kids understand what a word is when they experience what it does. When grown-ups depend on print for information and fun, kids see print as valuable. When grown-ups share tips about reading and writing, kids begin to crack the code. Literacy skills are best built on a strong foundation of print awareness. The activities in Chapter 3 promote print knowledge and power!

Wow! I'm Reading!

When is a child ready to read? Reading requires:

    phonemic awareness
    letter recognition
    print awareness

With this knowledge in place, most kids learn to read and write with ease, sometimes on their own.

What's the best method? Kids who are taught explicitly how our alphabetic code works consistently show the most achievement. Here's where phonics instruction plays an enormous role. Phonemic awareness gives kids the knowledge that words contain sound units. Phonics instruction teaches kids how those sound units link with letter symbols to record words — words that can be written or read. Phonics empowers kids to figure out what print says and to put their own words in print.

The phonics activities in Chapter 5 playfully add print to the phonemic-awareness experiences described in Chapter 2. With reading readiness confidently in place, it's an easy step to take. Kids who can blend spoken sounds like **c a t** into *cat* can now sound out printed words to read. Kids who can "unglue" words like *mom* into **m o m** can now use letters to represent each sound and spell.

The Write Stuff

Learning to write confirms to kids that print is communication. As natural communicators, kids are driven to write just as they are to speak. Kids begin their writing careers when crayons become useful as markers. Think of those first scribbles as printed babbles. Just as babbles start to sound more like words, scribbles begin to look more like letters. From random to refined, a child's writing develops into understandable communication in much the same way that his speech develops. Although there is a general order to writing development, kids move back and forth through stages as they experiment and explore print.

Writing boosts reading ability. Let's take a closer look at the invented spelling stage to see why. A child who invents the spelling "grl" for *girl* is clearly developing phonemic awareness. Grappling with the sound-letter link is critical phonics practice.

In print-rich homes, writing blossoms. With grown-ups who honor even those first scribbles as important messages, kids learn that writing is communication. The writing activities in Chapter 6 let kids experience writing as meaningful print.

The Rewards of Reading

Why read? What's in it for the child? Children need proof that reading is a worthwhile activity before they'll join in. Luckily, literacy is an easy sell. Just snuggle up with a good book and release the wondrous ideas so magically held in print for a child. After all, the goal of reading is not to sound out words but to unlock meaning. Kids need to understand where practicing reading skills will lead.

THE CHANGING CLASSROOM OR LITERACY LABS FOR LITTLE ONES

Learning letters in preschool? Reading in kindergarten? If you're wondering where the modeling clay is, look again. It's still there, but kids may be using it to form letters along with their pies! What's going on here?

Early literacy learning is critical: Kids who get off to a good start hang on to their advantage. Kids who don't, seldom recover. Those who fall behind in first grade rarely catch up to grade level ability.

But is early literacy learning developmentally appropriate? Yes, if the activities meet the needs and learning style of the child. Young children are hands-on, minds-on learners. So expect to see such materials as tactile letters, marker boards, alphabet puzzles, and beautiful books — not worksheets — in a preschool setting. Expect to hear the sounds of stories, songs, and rhymes resonating throughout the room. Expect to see print thoroughly explored and enjoyed.

Educators estimate it takes 1,000 "literacy lab" hours (see Putting It All Together described on page 12) with a caring adult before a child is ready to read. Early childhood educators are taking on the challenge by transforming classrooms into literacy labs. Here children can playfully discover the wonders of print and language.

Reading aloud is one of the best ways to connect kids to the rich rewards of reading. It transports kids to fantastic realms of fact and fiction long before they can read on their own. The world's rich heritage of folk tales, poetry, and literature is theirs. If volcanoes or insects are more to a little one's liking, books are there to deliver fascinating facts and information. Let kids hear you reading directions or a recipe aloud so they understand that reading opens practical worlds, too. Even deciphering junk mail, packaging, or road signs can be a motivator. What gives read-aloud text meaning? It's the wonderful experiences and the rich language you're offering to describe those experiences. Reading is most meaningful when a child can make a connection to her own life. See Chapter 1 for ways to build a foundation of conceptual knowledge and vocabulary.

Using text as a springboard for a child's creativity sharpens comprehension skills. Kids can retell a favorite tale by making their own puppet show or acting out what they would have done in the hero's shoes. Kids can report to the family on facts learned from a dinosaur book. Or, they can complete a craft from read-aloud directions. No comprehension test can check understanding better than a child's original responses to what was read. And there's a bonus: Using print to inspire kids to question, create, and connect makes reading vital to their lives. The activities in Chapter 7 offer ways to deepen understanding while sharing reading's rich rewards.

Putting It All Together

Literacy building requires weaving together all elements of language communication: thinking, listening, speaking, reading, and writing. So children continually need opportunities to explore these elements in a meaningful way.

Here's how a day of language exploration might look. A child starts out in the morning immersed in a pile of books, then moves on to scribbling with crayons and pens. A grown-up includes her in writing a shopping list. Once on the road, letters and words on signs they pass are pointed out, discussed, and read. Reading labels and identifying familiar products in the store is part of shopping; so is talking about all those delicious, colorful fruits and vegetables. They play rhyming games on the drive back. Next comes listening to a favorite nursery rhyme CD and singing together back home. A grown-up comments on the magazine he's reading while the child plays with alphabet magnets on the refrigerator door. The grand finale involves listening to a wonderful bedtime story read aloud.

The literacy-building activities in this book complement such a language-rich day. They help your child learn to read and write through playful yet effective exploration, games, and projects. When learning to read is this fun and meaningful, your child will not only be able to read, but love to read!

IT'S STANDARD!

STATE STANDARDS SAY...

Learning to read is key to a child's success in school … and life. Most folks agree that teaching such a critical skill cannot be haphazard. Educators, parents, and community members in most states have adopted comprehensive content standards for language arts instruction. These standards specify which skills children ought to have mastered by the end of each school year, from kindergarten through grade twelve. What children learn one year becomes the building block for the next, creating continuity between grade levels. The standards in the early grades set the foundation for proficiency in later years. Generally the expectation is that children will read fluently at their grade level, at least by third grade. Assessments (tests) are given so parents and teachers will know if children have met the standards and how to help those who have not.

The activities in this book help children meet the sort of rigorous standards set nationwide for beginning literacy. Reading readiness and beginning reading instruction now start in kindergarten, so examples of typical content standards for kindergarten language arts are presented throughout this book in the section State Standards Say …. For information on specific content standards in your state, visit the website of your State Department of Education.

This is fun!

LET'S TALK ABOUT IT!

Your mind is full of wonderful ideas. How can you share them? By using words! "Let's swing together!" "I'm hungry!" Each word means something — an action, an idea, an object.

Stringing words together makes a sentence. Talk to a friend: "I have a new ball." Then listen to what he or she says to you: "Hey, let's play soccer!" See how we share ideas with words?

COLLAGE COLLECTION

Make a collection of magazine pictures that are all in the same *category* (they are all alike in some way).
If you love pets, collect pictures of dogs, cats, fish, and birds. It's up to you because it's your collection!

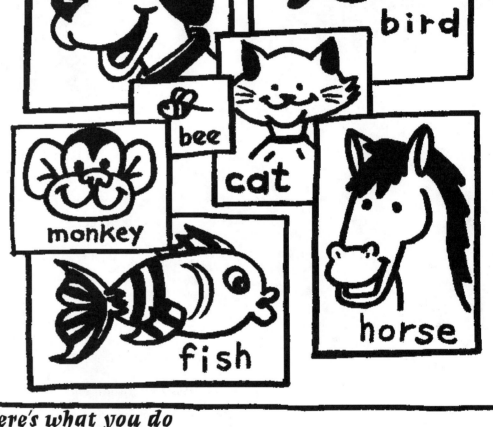

Here's what you need

Old magazines
Child safety scissors
Paste
Large sheet of paper or
    poster board

Here's what you do

1. Once you pick a category, hunt for matching pictures in the magazines. Cut them out and paste them on the paper. Ask a grown-up to help you label your pictures.

2. Pick a new category each time you make a Collage Collection. Save your collages in an album (page 110).

MOre Fun for YOU!

PLAY SORT YOUR SETS. Find four magazine pictures in the same category. Paste each picture on an index card. Make five sets of category cards. Mix them up. Can you sort them back into categories?

PLAY OPPOSITE PEOPLE. Magazines are filled with pictures of people. Fold a large sheet of paper in half. Sort pictures for one side or the other — People at Work/People at Play, Children/Grown-ups, Happy People/Sad People — and paste them on the paper.

PLAY BRAINSTORM. Think of a category: animals, foods, round things, red things, things that grow. Take turns brainstorming all words that fit that category.

PLAY BACKPACK. Play Bulging Backpack on page 41. This time everything must be in the same category. "Yes, a bike, a car, and a fire engine can be in my backpack, but not a chicken! Can you guess my category?"

Play Bulging Backpack on page 41.

READING ON

Share the ways these books categorize words and concepts: *What the Sun Sees* by Nancy Tafuri, *ABCDrive!* by Naomi Howland, and *What Makes Me Happy?* by Catherine and Laurence Anholt.

Teaching Time

Concept development is the basis for building vocabulary. Children naturally use *compare-and-contrast* as a strategy for developing concepts. Sorting objects helps children organize ideas by focusing on key elements that allow inclusion in or exclusion from the category.

Talking with a child about why a picture might be in one category but not another (or maybe in both) improves her ability to categorize by describing similarities and differences between objects.

STATE STANDARDS SAY...

Children will:
◆ identify and sort common words into basic categories.
◆ extend their vocabulary and conceptual knowledge.

SEQUENCE CROWN

How does your
day begin?
How does it end?
What happens
in between?

Here's what you do

1. Fold the paper lengthwise. Cut along the fold. Fold each piece in half again. Tape them together so they form one long strip.

2. Talk about what has happened and what will happen today. Draw a scene from your day in each of the four squares. Be sure the first square shows how you begin and the last square shows how you end your day. In the other two squares, draw two activities from the middle of the day. A grown-up can label each scene in your own words.

3. Ask a grown-up to fit the strip around your head and tape the ends together. Retell the story of your day, pointing to each picture.

Here's what you need

Sheet of white paper
Child safety scissors
Tape
Markers

More Fun for You!

MAKE A SEQUENCE CROWN.
Show seasons of the year, daytime to night, or caterpillar to moth. Adjust the number of squares to the event.

READING ZONE

Day to night. Spring to summer. Nature is full of sequence changes. Read about them in *The Goodnight Circle* by Carolyn Lesser and *Night is Coming* by W. Nikola-Lisa. To practice retelling in sequence, say, "Grandma didn't hear that book we read last night. Can you tell her the story?"

Teaching Time

A key to comprehension is *sequence.* Without understanding the concept of first, middle, and last, a child cannot understand the plot in a tale or how to follow directions.

STATE STANDARDS SAY...

Children will:
◆ retell familiar stories.
◆ relate an experience or creative story in a logical sequence.

MAKE AN ACCORDION BOOK.
Show an event with many scenes.

MAKE A STORYBOARD.
Leave the strip flat and use it to retell your favorite story by drawing scenes from the story, beginning to end, in the squares. Point to the pictures as you retell your favorite stories and events.

1-2-3 AND DO!

It's fun to make a cool craft by following directions.
Ask a grown-up to read these directions to you.
Look at the pictures. Can you follow the steps?

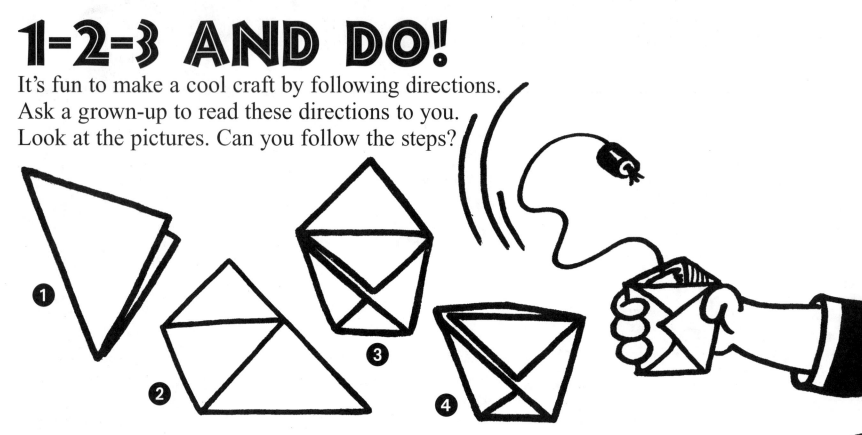

Here's what you need
8½" x 8½" (21.25 x 21.25 cm) square
  of paper

Here's what you do
1. Fold your paper in half.
2. Place the point of the triangle
away from you. Fold each corner to
the opposite side.
3. Fold one top edge down.
4. Flip the paper over and do the
same fold on the other side. Use
your hands to open the shape.
Presto! You made a cup.

MORE FUN FOR YOU!

MAKE A BASKET. Tape a narrow strip of paper to both sides of the cup to form a handle. Decorate your basket with markers.

MAKE A GAME. Knot a bead on one end of a 12" (30 cm) piece of string. Tape the other end to the inside of the cup. Toss the bead into the air. Can you catch it in the cup? What fun!

MAKE A HAT. Make the cup from a sheet of newspaper. Decorate it with markers. Turn it upside down and wear it on your head. You look great!

Teaching Time

Children follow directions every day. For many emergent readers, the realization that reading opens up the world of cooking, making things, and playing new games is a big motivator. "Wow! I'm reading!" can quickly be followed by "Wow! Reading helped me do it myself!"

STATE STANDARDS SAY...

Children will:
◆ understand and follow one- and two-step oral directions.
◆ develop the language of schooling.
◆ learn to listen attentively.

WHAT AM I?

Here's a fun game! A grown-up or older child reads one clue at a time while you listen carefully. Can you guess what I am? Draw your guess, changing it with each new clue. Take turns making up WHAT AM I? clues.

Here's what you need

Paper
Crayons

Here's what you do

1. Fold the paper into four sections.

2. Listen carefully to the first clue. Draw what you think I am in the first section.

3. Now listen to clue two. You will probably need to change your guess. Draw what you think I am now.

4. Make changes with each clue you hear. After you've heard all four clues, is your guess correct?

"WHAT AM I?" CLUES

1. I am something that keeps you warm.
2. I am something you wear.
3. Actually, there are two of me.
4. You put me on your hands.
What am I? Gloves or mittens!

1. I am alive.
2. I grow from the ground.
3. I am taller than you.
4. Birds make their nests in me.
What am I? A tree!

1. I go fast.
2. I have two wheels.
3. I can take you from place to place.
4. I don't have a motor.
What am I? A bicycle!

Now, make up your own **WHAT AM I?** clues for others to guess!

WHAT'S NEXT?

When you listen to an exciting story, don't you wonder what will happen next? That's just what good readers do! They make a *prediction* (best guess) about what is going to happen. Then, they read on to find out if they were right!

Here's what you need
....

An engaging storybook

Here's what you do
....

1. Look at the front cover and title. What do you think the story will be about?

2. A grown-up reads sections of the story, stopping before each exciting part. Consider the new information. Look at the pictures, too. What do you think will happen next? It's fine to change your prediction as you gather more information.

3. Now read the ending. Was your prediction like or unlike the ending? (It doesn't matter. The fun part is reading on to see what happens.)

These fun tales are great prediction practice: *The Runaway Bunny* by Margaret Wise Brown, *Caps for Sale* by Esphyr Slobodkina, *Blueberries for Sal* by Robert McCloskey, and *What Baby Wants* by Phyllis Root.

READING ZONE

Teaching Time

Reading revolves around making predictions. Prediction propels us forward as we read on to discover the outcome.

Making predictions during a read-aloud story promotes active engagement with the story and deeper comprehension, even before a child is able to read on her own. You also show respect for her ideas.

STATE STANDARDS SAY...

Children will: use pictures and context to make predictions about story content.

WRITE MY WORDS

Share your thoughts and ideas — then watch as they become printed words on a page!

Here's what you need

Paper and pencil or pen

Here's what you do

Tell a story to a grown-up.

◆ Talk about a special place you visited.

◆ Say what you like about your friend.

◆ Describe what makes you happy, mad, or sad.

◆ Tell all you know about something that really interests you.

◆ Retell your favorite story.

Watch as the grown-up carefully writes down your words as you talk.

Now, read your story together!

Here's what a grown-up does

◆ Write down the child's exact words (no editing, please!). Print legibly.

◆ Encourage him to say more about the topic by asking open-ended questions.

◆ Think of a title together and credit the author (by Jason).

◆ As you enthusiastically reread the story together, point to each word. Share basic print concepts: "See how I write and read from left to right and from top to bottom? Words are made from letters. See how I leave spaces between my words? See the period at the end of each sentence?"

◆ Give the child a chance to read the story on his own, pointing to each word.

MOre FuN foR YOu!

ILLUSTRATE YOUR STORY. Use crayons or markers. Try copying a few words underneath the grown-up's writing.

DATE THE STORIES. Store them in an album to reread from time to time.

ALBUM

And then we went to the lake.

Writing down a child's speech verbatim is called a *Language Experience Story.* Reading their words back proves the usefulness of written language. "That's my story, exactly as I told it. We can read it again!"

Looking closely at the story allows you to share important print concepts: the difference between letters and words, the purpose of simple punctuation marks, and the progression of the text.

STATE STANDARDS SAY...

Children will:
◆ share information and ideas in complete, coherent sentences.
◆ dictate messages and stories for others to write.
◆ describe common objects and events in both general and specific language.
◆ follow words from left to right and from top to bottom on the printed page.
◆ recognize that sentences in print are made up of separate words.
◆ distinguish letters from words.
◆ understand that printed materials provide information.

START WITH SOUNDS

Shhh! Don't say a word. Close your eyes and just listen! What do you hear? Your dog barking? A computer humming? Eggs sizzling? Sounds are all around!

Now say your name. You just made a super sound! Say it again very slowly — do you notice several sounds hidden in your name?

Ready to explore more sounds? Well then, let the sound fun start!

RHYME TIME

Did you ever have a time when you couldn't make a rhyme? Not with these fun games. You'll go rhyme crazy!

tall
ball
fall

THUMBS UP!

A grown-up says three words. Put your thumbs up if they all rhyme. Thumbs down if they don't. Here we go!

◆ man, can, fan
◆ go, no, stop
◆ fish, dish, wish
◆ bike, hike, run
◆ candy, dandy, carrot

Can you think of your own rhyming words to play Thumbs Up! with your friends?

IMAGINE

A grown-up says a silly sentence with a missing word. Use rhyming clues to help you figure out the missing word. (Note: Please don't write in this book. Thank you!)

◆ Imagine a bear, with long brown (What rhymes with bear? Hair!)
◆ Imagine a mouse, in an itty, bitty _____?_____. (What rhymes with mouse? House!)
◆ Imagine a flea, drinking some _____?_____. (Tea!)
◆ Imagine a cat, with a baseball and _____?_____. (Bat!)
◆ Image a whale with a flippy-floppy _____?_____. (Tail!)

Think of your own silly sentence. A good way to start is to imagine your own silly critter.

NURSERY RHYMES

For nursery rhyme fun, try these games:

Listen and learn nursery rhymes.
A grown-up can read them aloud to you, or you can hear them on a tape or CD. They're fun to chant.

A grown-up says most of the rhyme.
Can you use rhyming clues to think of the missing word?

Hickory, dickory dock
The mouse ran up the _____?_____ (clock).

Jack and Jill
Went up the _____?_____ (hill).

Up above the world so high,
Like a diamond in the _____?_____ (sky).

Say a rhyme along with a grown-up.
Clap when you hear a rhyming word.

Make up your own version —
the sillier, the better!

Twinkle, twinkle little star.
Take a ride in my new car.
Up and down the roads we'll go.
Through the mud and through the snow.
Twinkle, twinkle little star.
Take a ride in my new car.

BE A RHYME

Give yourself a rhyming name. Invite your family, friends, and pets to join in the fun for a day:
"Hello, Mom Rom and Glad Dad. Today, I'm Jason Pason and this is my dog, Bowser Wowser!"

clap
clap

CLAP, CLAP, PAT

Practice this pattern by clapping your hands, then patting your knees: Clap, clap, pat. When you can do it easily, take turns with a grown-up or around a circle of kids, saying rhyming words on the pat. They can be real words or made-up words, as long as they rhyme:
Clap, clap, pat ("frog"). Clap, clap, pat ("clog"). Clap, clap, pat ("log").

SING ALL ABOUT IT!

Sing rhyming jingles to the tune of "Oh, Do You Know the Muffin Man?"

Oh, have you seen,
A frog on a log?
A frog on a log?
A frog on a log?
Oh, have you seen
A frog on a log?
Quite a sight to see!

Try these verses to get you started.
Then, make up your own!

A bug in a jug
A bee in a tree
A fish on a dish

Try fancy versions, too.

Oh, have you seen
A man in a can,
Riding in a van,
To buy a frying pan?
Oh, have you seen
A man in a can?
Quite a sight to see!

Enjoy these beautiful editions of classic nursery rhymes: *My Very First Mother Goose* and *Here Comes Mother Goose,* edited by Iona Opie and illustrated by Rosemary Wells. The large text also allows you to share print concepts with a child.

Teaching Time

Children are naturally attracted to rhymes and jingles. They'll often repeat familiar chants as they play. Rhyming games are a perfect way to introduce awareness that words have sounds — sounds that have similar patterns. And the silliness of rhyming is the perfect chance to share laughter along with language learning.

STATE STANDARDS SAY...

Children will: recite poems, rhymes, and songs.

RHYMING TREASURE HUNT

Making rhymes is so much fun, especially when you collect rhymes for super stuff around your home.

Go on a rhyming treasure hunt and save your finds in collection bags!

Here's what you need

Household objects
Large zippered plastic bag • Markers
Magazines • Child safety scissors

Here's what you do

1. Find two things in your home with rhyming names — like a shoe and a jar of glue. Place them in a bag and keep collecting. You can add something blue; how about the number two?

2. Now add pictures from a magazine — stew! Use markers to draw your own pictures — a zoo!

3. Say the words for each object in your bag. Can you hear a sound pattern?

More Fun for You!

RHYME CHALLENGE. Set a rhyming collection before a friend. Challenge her to think of how each object rhymes with the next: shoe, blue … paste? "Hmmm, it must be glue! Two, stew … why the picture of a cow? Oh, it says, moo!"

TOSS-A-RHYME. Sit in a circle with a group of kids. Pick a favorite object such as a ball. Think of a rhyme and say, "ball, wall." Toss it to a friend. He must think of a rhyme such as "ball, crawl." Nonsense words like "ball, flall" are fine, too. Pick a new object to rhyme when you're all rhymed out!

RHYME SORT. Dump out stuff from two or three rhyme bags. Mix up the objects. Can you sort them back into their rhyming groups?

SYLLABLE SAM

This funny puppet breaks words into chunks. Can you help him? Can you put the words back together? Listening carefully to the sounds in words helps you learn to read and write.

Er-i-ka

Here's what you need

8½" x 11" (21.25 x 27.5 cm) sheet of paper
Markers
Child safety scissors
Paper scraps
Paste

Here's what you do

1. Fold the paper into thirds lengthwise. Flip over the folded strip and fold it in half as shown.
2. Fold the ends back to meet the center fold.
3. Draw lips and eyes on the puppet. Cut out paper hair and ears and paste on.
4. Place your fingers into the top slot and your thumb into the bottom to make Syllable Sam speak.

To play:

Ask a grown-up to have Sam slowly say your name. Watch how many times Sam closes his mouth to say your name. Clap along with the mouth movements. Put your fingers in the air to show how many syllables (sound chunks) there are in your name.

MORe FUN FOR YOU!

Count the syllables in the names of your friends, favorite foods, or any special words while Sam says them.

Try these different ways to mark syllable sounds: Slap a table, tap two pens together, or jump as Sam says each syllable.

SYLLABLE SMOOSH. A grown-up and Syllable Sam challenge you to put together two-syllable words:

Grown-up: "flash"
You: "light"
Together: "flashlight!"

Grown-up: "pic"
You: "nic"
Together: "picnic!"

SYLLABLE SORT. Gather toys and objects or magazine pictures. Have a grown-up write 1, 2, and 3+ on index cards. Clap each word and sort by number of syllables.

1	2	3+
cap	pencil	overalls
cork	paper	sunglasses
spoon	Lego	banana

MONSTER MUNCH

Watch out. This monster is a picky eater. Listen carefully and you'll know just what to feed him.

Here's what you need

Paste
Sheet of white paper
Large empty cereal box
Child safety scissors
Markers
Construction paper
Small toys and objects
Index cards
Magazines

Here's what you do

Make your monster:
1. With a grown-up, paste the paper on the front of the cereal box. Cut a large mouth hole through the paper and cardboard.
2. Draw a monster face.
3. Paste huge construction-paper ears to the side panels. This monster is a careful listener!

Feed your monster:
1. A grown-up offers you some strange "monster food," such as a cap, a car, a pen, a Lego, or a ball. Then, she starts feeding the monster by dropping, say, the pen, in its mouth as she says "pen." Now, you know that today your monster will only eat things that start with the **p** sound. Pens, paper, and pennies are yummy, but a cap or ball is not!
2. If your monster is extra-hungry, use index cards to draw your own pictures or paste on magazine pictures for more **p** words.
3. When the feeding is finished, dump out the objects. Now you say each word and listen for the same starting sounds.

More Fun for You!

SOUND HUNT. Need more monster food? Have a grown-up help you pick and paste a magazine picture to the front of a paper bag. If you've chosen a photo of a car, then you need to search for objects that start with that same **c** sound: cap, can, card, or candy (but not cereal).

SAME-SOUND BAGS. Save the monster food to create same-sound collections. Follow instructions for Rhyming Treasure Hunt on page 34, but instead of items that rhyme, create collection bags of stuff that starts with the same sound. Play the More Fun for You! games on page 35, but this time, match objects with names that start the same.

IN THE END. Time for a change of diet! Now your monster prefers objects with names that *end* with the same sound … tricky, tricky! And picky, picky monster! But you won't be fooled. If **n** is the target sound, then pen, crayon, green, can, mitten are fine, but not a top or a book.

These books are full of same-sound tongue twisters: *Apples, Alligators, and Also Alphabets* by Odette and Bruce Johnson, *Animalia* by Graeme Base, and *Dr. Seuss's ABC*.

Teaching Time — The first phoneme in a word is the easiest to identify. So focusing a child's attention on beginning sounds is a great way to introduce the concept that words are composed of phonemes. When words with the same beginning sound can be matched with ease, turn the child's attention to the more difficult task of identifying ending sounds.

STATE STANDARDS SAY...

Children will: track and identify the number, sameness/difference and order of isolated phonemes.

STARTING SOUNDS, ENDING SOUNDS!

These games and songs will really sharpen your listening skills. Sometimes tune into the beginning sounds. Sometimes tune into the ending sounds. Don't be tricked!

TONGUE TWISTERS

Say crazy tongue twisters with a grown-up:

Seven silly snakes snacked on snails.

Bouncing blue bubbles blew backward.

Dancing dinos dined on delicious doughnuts.

Can you make up your own?

Dancing dinos dined on delicious doughnuts.

NAME-SOUND SONG

Sing this to the tune of "Have You Ever Seen a Lassie?"

Does your name begin with **d**, with **d**, with **d**?
If your name begins with **d**
Then stand up right now!
There's Daniel, and Donovan, and Dylana, and David.
If your name begins with **d**
Then stand up right now!

◆ Now do the same with ending sounds.

NEAT-O-NAMES

Be someone extra special by adding a same-sound word to your name: Terrific Tara, Amazing Amanda, Jazzy James, Dizzy Danica. Make silly names for everyone in your family and class at school.

BULGING BACKPACK

Take turns with a grown-up saying, "I'm going on a hike. And in my backpack are a radio and a reindeer. What else can I bring along?"
"A raisin?" "Sure."
"A rainbow?" "You bet."
"A shoe?" "No way!"

◆ Play again, listening for words that have different starting sounds.

◆ Pack items with the same ending sounds, like *kite, mat,* and *jet.*

SILLY SARAH LOVES TO SAY

Sing to the tune of "Old MacDonald":

Silly Sarah loves to say,
Sandwich, spider, snake.
Silly Sarah loves to say,
Sandwich, spider, snake.
With an **S S** here and an **S S** there.
Here an **S**, there an **S**.
Everywhere an **S S**.
Silly Sarah loves to say,
Sandwich, spider, snake!

◆ Now, try the song with these same-ending-sound words:

Our ending sounds are all the same,
Kitten, chicken, ten.
Our ending sounds are all the same,
Kitten, chicken, ten.
With an **n n** here and an **n n** there.
Here an **n**, there an **n**.
Everywhere an **n n**.
Our ending sounds are all the same,
Kitten, chicken, ten.

BLEND IT!

Uh-oh! These words came "unglued." Can you blend them back together? Be sure to use letter sounds, not letter names (**"mmm,"** not "em").

SLOW TALK

A grown-up stretches out words with his voice. Can you figure out these weird-sounding words?

SHIVER WORDS
Grown-up: **b-b-b** … ed … You: bed
Grown-up: **c-c-c** … andy … You: candy
Grown-up: **d-d-d** … inosaur … You: dinosaur

AMAZING ECHO
Grown-up shouts: **p** … an … You echo: pan
Grown-up shouts: **t** … elephone … You echo: telephone
Grown-up shouts: sto … **p** … You echo: stop
Grown-up shouts: balloo … **n** … You echo: balloon

BLEND AND DO

Listen, figure out the action, then do it! **s-i-t, r-u-n, c-l-a-p, j-u-m-p, h-o-p**

SNAIL SPEAK

A grown-up can help you draw the snail on this page onto an index card. First, listen to a grown-up speak like a slowpoke. As she says a word in slow motion, move your finger over the snail's body, from left to right, starting at the head. Say the word when you reach the end. Grown-up: **p-o-t** … You: **pot!**

SOUND-SONGS

Sing along to the tune of "Are You Sleeping?" Can you guess the word?

m- a- t, **m- a- t**.
What's the word
That you heard?
m- a- t, **m- a- t**.
I said mat.
I said mat.

◆ Sing to the tune of "Oh, Do You Know the Muffin Man?"

The sounds in my word say
f- a- n, f- a- n, f- a- n.
The sounds in my word say **f- a- n.**
Can you guess my word? **Fan!**
(shout)

Teaching Time

A child may correctly say **m-a-n**, but still not recognize these sounds as a word. Children must be able to connect phonemes, then recognize what they hear as a familiar word.

Each of these games can be adapted to any level of difficulty. Tasks are listed here from easiest to most challenging:
1. compound word parts: cow … boy, cowboy (Syllable Smoosh, page 37)
2. syllables: pen … cil, pencil (Syllable Smoosh, page 37)
3. the first sound with all the others: **b** … ag, bag (Shiver Words, page 42)
4. all but the last sound plus the last sound: mea … **t** (Amazing Echo, page 42)
5. each sound: **c-l-a-p**, clap (Blend and Do)

Children will: blend vowel-consonant sounds orally to make words or syllables.

STATE STANDARDS SAY…

UNGLUE IT!

Listen carefully. Can you "unglue" words, down to their smallest sound parts? Play these games and give it a try.

SOUND SNAKE

Draw a snake on a strip of cardboard. Be sure its head is on the left end and its tail is on the right. Cut out the snake and place it before you.

A grown-up will give you a *target sound* and a penny. If you hear that target sound at the beginning of the word, place the penny on the snake's head.

If you hear that sound at the end, place the penny on the tail.

If you hear the sound in the middle, place the penny on the snake's belly.

◆ The target sound is **d**:
dog (beginning)
mad (end)
puddle (middle)

◆ The target sound is **g**:
got (beginning)
dog (end)
wagon (middle)

◆ The target sound is **b**:
ball (beginning)
cab (end)
table (middle)

PENNY PUSH-UPS

A grown-up can make you a sound card with two side-by-side circles by tracing around a penny. Set two pennies on the card and be ready to push them up into the circles.

Slowly repeat the word a grown-up says, sliding a penny into the circle for each sound you hear.

up: **u-p**
off: **o-ff**
go: **g-o**

◆ For a challenge, use three circles and three coins:

can: **c-a-n**
book: **b-o o-k**
read: **r-ē-d**

◆ How about listening for four sounds?

fast: **f-a-s-t**
drive: **d-r-i-v**
pigs: **p-i-g-s**

BUBBLE GUM WORDS

Pretend you are chewing on a bubble gum word. As soon as it's soft and stretchy, slowly pull it out of your mouth. As you pull it away from your lips, say the word in slow motion, so you can hear each sound. As soon as the word is all the way out, clap your hands and quickly say the word: **w-e-t** (clap) **wet!**

Segmenting is a prerequisite to spelling. In order for a child to spell *hot*, he must be able to break the word into the phonemes **h-o-t**.

Teaching Time

Each of the Unglue It! games can be adapted to any level of difficulty. Tasks are listed here from easiest to most challenging. Instead of you segmenting the word for the child to blend together, the child identifies and segments words into

1. syllables: ca … mel, *camel* (Syllable Smoosh, page 37)
2. beginning sounds: **r** accoon, *raccoon* (Shiver Words, page 42)
3. ending sounds: racoo **n**, *raccoon* (Amazing Echo, page 42)
4. middle vowel sound: m-**o**-p, *mop* (Sound Snake and Push-Ups, pages 44-45)
5. Each sound: **f-a-s-t**, *fast* (Blend and Do, page 43).

STATE STANDARDS SAY...

Children will:
◆ learn that spoken language is composed of sequences of sounds.
◆ learn to segment and identify the sounds in spoken words.
◆ distinguish one-syllable words and separate into beginning or ending sounds.

SWITCH-A-ROO

The fun thing about the sounds in words is that they can be moved every which way: You can add sounds, take them away, or switch them around. Make new words. Make crazy unwords. It's up to you!

MYSTERY RHYME

It rhymes with men. It starts with **t**.
("men," "t … en," "ten!")

It rhymes with log. It starts with **d**.
("log," "d … og," "dog!")

It rhymes with go. It starts with **n**.
("go," "n … o," "no!")

It rhymes with sun. It starts with **f**.
("sun," "f … un," "fun!")

It rhymes with look. It starts with **b**.
("look," "b … ook," "book!")

MIX-UP

Use rhyming clues to guess what a grown-up really means:

We ride in a jar. (A what? A car.)
In the morning, I comb my bear.
(That's silly! My hair.)
I sleep in a sled. (bed)
I drink goose. (juice)
Bounce my doll. (ball)
Now you make up a mixed-up sentence for a grown-up to guess.

SING SILLY SOUNDS!

Sing to the tune of "Zippity Doo Dah." Pick a sound and change all the Zippity Doo Dahs so they start with that sound:

Rippity Roo Rah, Rippity Ray
r r r
Is the sound that I say.
Rippity Roo Rah, Rippity Ray
r r r
Is the sound that I say.

◆ Sing many silly verses: Sippity Soo Sah, Nippity Noo Nah — do all your favorite sounds!

Sippity Soo Sah, Nippity Noo Nah

WHAT'S MISSING?

If your mom is "Om" and your dad is "Ad", it must be Missing Sound Day. Can you figure out what a grown-up wants if he says, "Bring me an:
encil." (pencil)
up." (cup)
ork." (fork)
ubber band." (rubber band)
Make up your own missing-sound words!

T-TALK

Pick a sound of the day, like **t**. All your friends and family members must change their names to start with **t**:
Tom (Mom), Tad (Dad), Tohn (John), Tephanie (Stephanie).

◆ Can you make more **t** words? How about foods? Don't you think teanut tutter and telly or tilk and tookies are tunny tacks?

Switch sounds and change words with these silly tales: *Don't Forget the Bacon!* by Pat Hutchins, *Jamberrry* by Bruce Degen, and *There's a Wocket in my Pocket!* by Dr. Seuss.

Teaching Time

Sound manipulation teaches children that language is fluid. Children must hold phonemic knowledge in their memory as they make each change. Tasks include:
Syllable changes
◆ Say *cowboy* without the "cow." (boy)
◆ Say *cowboy* without the "boy" and with "girl" instead. (cowgirl)
◆ Say *jumping* without the "ing." (jump)
Phoneme changes
◆ Say *cat* without the **c**. (at)
◆ Say *nose* without the **z**. (no)
◆ Say *tap* without the **p** and with **n** instead. (tan)
◆ Say *tip* without the **i** and with **o** instead. (top)

STATE STANDARDS SAY...

Children will: track and identify changes in simple syllables and words as one sound is added, substituted, omitted, shifted, or repeated.

PRINT POWER!

Look around!
What do you see?

Words!

Listen. What do you hear?

Words!

Speak. What do you say?

Words!

Words are everywhere!
It's fun to write words, read
words, and play with words.
Discover just how important
words are as you capture some
on paper, on cards, and in crafts
and games.

MY NAME GAMES

What's in a name?
Lots of fun if it's yours!

RAINBOW WRITING

Ask a grown-up to print your name nice and big with a marker (using a capital for the first letter only). See how only these letters form your name? Now you trace around the letters over and over with different colored markers. Soon your name will look as colorful as a rainbow.

LETTER LINEUP

Write your name on a strip of paper. Cut apart the letters. Mix them up. Can you paste them down in order?

SING B-I-N-G-O WITH YOUR NAME!

There was a boy who had a dog
(had green eyes, brown hair, tan shoes …)
And Cody was his name-O
C - O - D - Y
C - O - D - Y
C - O - D - Y
And Cody was his name-O!

ME COLLAGE

Look for the letters of your name in the words on magazine pages. Cut out the letters and paste them down in order on bright construction paper. Now look for words and pictures that tell about you. Cut these out and paste them around your name.

AUTOGRAPH, PLEASE?

Collect the printed names of friends and family members.
Do they look like yours? How are they different?
The best place to collect names is in your
very own autograph book.

Here's what you need

2 sheets of white paper
Child safety scissors
Hole punch
Sheet of construction paper
Yarn or ribbon

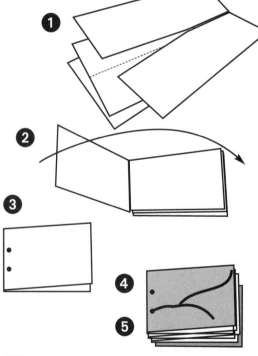

Here's what you do

Make it!
1. Cut the white paper in half the long way.
2. Fold each piece in half and stack.
3. A grown-up can help you punch two holes near the fold of each sheet.
4. Cut a piece of construction paper in half the long way for the cover. Fold it in half. Place the paper sheets inside. Punch holes in the same spots on the construction paper.
5. Thread yarn or ribbon through the holes. Fold the binding as shown.

Use it!
◆ Collect signatures, messages, and art meant especially for you from friends and family members.
◆ To gather lots of signatures, bring your autograph book along to parties and get-togethers.
◆ Don't forget to have your friends sign in when they come to play.

MOre FUn for YOU!

FAMILY PHOTO FUN.
Use a photo album with two slots per page. In the top slot, put a photo of a favorite person. Ask a grown-up to print the person's name on an index card and put that in the slot below. Fill the album for some fun reading!

NAME SORTS. Collect names on strips of paper. Try these ways of sorting the stack:

◆ by the beginning or ending letters

◆ by the number of letters in each name

◆ by the number of syllables in each name (see pages 36-37)

SET THE TABLE.
Plan this special dinner!
Invitations. Have a grown-up help you write "Come eat at 6:00" on the inside of folded sheets of paper.

You and the cook can sign your names below. Write the name of each family member on the front. Decorate with drawings of foods.
Place cards. Fold index cards in half. Write the name of a family member on each one. Decorate and set one at each person's place.

SPECIAL WORDS

Tangerine, love, I, Stegosaurus, pizza!
Long or short, words are fun to read and write! Collect special words. After you've built up a good supply, you can play these fun games. To store your words, cover a small box with colored paper and decorate it in your own special way.

FAVORITE WORD CARDS

Each day, write one favorite word on a card. Draw a picture of the word underneath or on the back.

Where can you find interesting words? In all these places:

Stories: pigs, wolf, bricks, sticks, straw, huff, puff

Kitchen: banana, marshmallow, lemon

Backyard or park: leaves, roots, bug, rock, creek

WORD SORT

How many ways can you sort your words? Grab a bundle of word cards and sort by:

Type
   Animals, foods, toys
   Actions and things
   Things indoors and outdoors

Sound
   Starting sounds
   Ending sounds
   Number of syllables
   Make up your own way to sort!

MATH, PAIRS, AND RECALL

Make a second word card (or a separate picture card) for 10 of your favorite words. Now you can use these 20 cards to play matching games. In each game, you can match a word to the same word, or a word to its picture. Take turns until all pairs are matched.

MATCH. Spread out cards for 10 different words. Stack the other 10 in a pile, face down. Take turns picking a card and placing it beneath the matching word before you.

PAIRS. Deal all cards between you and a friend. Set aside pairs within your hand. Take turns drawing cards from each other. If it's a match, set the pair aside.

RECALL. Spread out all cards face down. Take turns flipping over two cards at a time. If they match, keep the pair and take another turn. If not, turn the cards face down again.

SILLY SENTENCES

Think of a sentence as putting words together to tell a little story:

T. rex eats a lollipop on top of a beach ball.

Can you make sentences that use several of your favorite words? Lay out the word cards in order, leaving a space between each word. (Have a grown-up help you write any extra words you need.) Draw a picture of your silly sentence. Can you copy the sentence?

Teaching Time

Let the words a child loves to say be the special words he learns to read and write first. These special words are charged with exciting meaning, making them fun and easy to learn. Capturing words on cards sensitizes children to how words function as distinct units of language. Point out how letters combine to make meaningful words and how words combine to make meaningful sentences.

Children will:
◆ distinguish letters from words.
◆ recognize that sentences in print are made up of separate words.

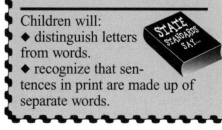

WORDWEAR

Wonderful words are everywhere. A word necklace is the perfect way to collect and show off your favorites. Start with a necklace strung with words all about you!

Here's what you need

Colorful markers
Index cards
Child safety scissors
Hole punch
Yarn

Here's what you do

1. Draw a picture of yourself on an index card. Write your name across the bottom.

2. Cut two index cards in half lengthwise. Snip the top corners and punch a hole at the top of each card. On each one, write a word that tells something about you (your age, how you feel, your favorite color, food, or pet). Your words might be: happy, girl, 4 years, purple.

3. Place your picture in the center and words on either side. Knot cards in place along a yard of yarn.

4. Wear your word necklace proudly. Can you read your words to curious friends?

MORe FUN FOR YOU!

Follow steps 1 to 3 to assemble these other necklace creations.

ANIMALS. Draw a picture of your favorite animal on the index card. Write its name across the bottom. On more cards, write words that tell something about that animal. Fish, for example, might be: water, fins, swims, gills; tortoise might be: shell, green, desert, slow.

CATEGORY FUN. Collect words from a magazine to display a special category. For example, glue food words on one side of each card and the matching food picture on the other.

BRAND-NAME LOTTO

Can you recognize *McDonald's, Cheerios,* or *Kool-Aid?* You may know that one means a burger, one is a cereal, and one is a drink. But have you ever thought about them as words? Look carefully — do you recognize any of the letters? Put those letters together and you've got a word. It's a word that says there's something yummy in store for you!

Here's what you need

Child safety scissors
Magazines or package labels
Paste
Index cards
Markers

Here's what you do

1. Cut out two examples of eight favorite brand names.
2. Paste each onto an index card. A grown-up can print the word beneath the logo.
3. Use your Brand-Name Cards to play Match, Pairs, and Recall (see page 55).

MORE FUN for YOU!

LETTER OR WORD? Use a ballpoint pen to circle letter after letter in old magazines and newspapers. Chant "letter, letter, letter" as you circle each one.

Now use a thin, red marker to circle words. Chant "word, word, word" as you circle each one. How can you tell if it's a word? It has spaces on either side. And it's almost always made of several letters!

LETTER OF THE DAY. Use a pen to circle a target letter, such as **n.** Circle all you can find, lowercase and uppercase. Chant **"n, n, n"** as you circle each one.

POINT IT OUT.

◆ Make the pointer on page 72. Use it to read around your home and school. Ask a grown-up to help you read the words you point to.

◆ With a clipboard and pencil in hand, you can write around your home or school, too. Copy some interesting looking words. A grown-up can help you figure out what they say.

LABEL MANIA. There can never be too many words in your home. Why not add some more? Ask a grown-up to help you label your world. She can write words like *door, refrigerator, table,* or *window* on sticky notes. You can stick them to the right spot. Then, read them as you walk by!

See the power of real-world print in these books: *I Read Signs* by Tana Hoban and *Oh, How I Wished I Could Read!* by John Gile.

Teaching Time
It's a good thing that print fills our environment. It makes it easy to create a literacy lesson anywhere, anytime. Point out the letters in familiar logos. Kids will likely recognize the difference between McDonald's and Burger King. But "think aloud" and show your child how to focus on the letters for information. Say, for example, "I'm looking for McDonald's. That word starts with the letter **B.** It says, **B B** Burger King. It can't be McDonald's. Oh, there's a giant **M.** That letter says **M M M.** That must be McDonald's."

Children will:
◆ understand that printed materials provide information.
◆ identify types of everyday printed materials.

READ-ALOUD PRINT POWER

There's so much to learn about print with a grown-up guide.

Here's what you need
....

A book with large print

Teaching Time

Here's how to guide a child through the conventions of print. Model each task; then, it's your child's turn.

◆ Point out the front cover, back cover, title page, table of contents, title, author, and illustrator.

◆ Track the print with your finger as you read, moving from word to word. Explain how there are spaces between words. Explain how you follow words from left to right and from top to bottom on the page.

◆ Frame (using your fingers or two tiny colored cards): one letter, two letters, one word, two words, an uppercase letter, a lowercase letter.

Understanding print concepts makes reading instruction effective. Make no assumptions with a beginning reader. Think aloud as you share all you know about print. Matching spoken words to print (tracking) and being able to distinguish letters from words are critical reading readiness skills.

Teaching Time

Children will:
◆ identify the front cover, back cover, and title page of a book.
◆ locate the title, table of contents, name of author, and name of illustrator.
◆ follow words from left to right and from top to bottom on the printed page.
◆ recognize that sentences in print are made up of separate words.
◆ distinguish letters from words.

STATE STANDARDS SAY...

LET'S PRETEND WITH PRINT

Read a menu; write a prescription; buy a ticket. Pretend play is even more fun and grown-up when you add print. So ask a grown-up to help you collect these print props.

Restaurant
Menus, recipe books, order pads, play money, signs, posters.

Travel agency, airport, bus, or train station
Tickets, schedules, travel brochures and guides, maps, postcards, travel posters, play money, luggage tags, magazines, books.

Health clinic, veterinary center, or dental center
Eye chart, health brochures, invoices, clipboard, pencils, appointment cards, calendar, magazines and books for the waiting room.

Museum, art gallery
Brochures, labels for pieces, price tags, art and object books, tickets, signs.

Grocery store, bakery
Signs, labels, product containers, advertisements, coupons, receipts, bags with logos, play money.

Theater, movie house, television studio
Tickets, play money, programs, posters, scripts, exit/enter signs.

TALK-AND-TELL CELL PHONE

You can take your cell phone any-where and use it to talk, talk, talk!

Here's what you need:

Scissors
7" (17.5 cm) cardboard tube
Paste
2" x 3½" (5 x 9 cm) piece of
   cardboard
Marker
Drinking straw
Tape

Here's what you do:

1. A grown-up can help you cut a 2½" x 1½" (6 x 4 cm) slit from each end of the tube. Push the center section flat.

2. Draw a number pad, like the one shown here, on the cardboard piece and paste it in the center section.

3. Cut a drinking straw in half. Tape it on to look like an antenna. Draw speaker "holes" at both ends.

Discover why print is so important in *I Like Books* by Anthony Browne and *Edward and the Pirates* by David McPhail.

Teaching Time
Print props are the perfect way for kids to explore literacy. After all, print is a vital part of the adult world they love to imitate. Dramatic play is a wonderful way for children to develop oral language. By adding print to dramatic play, kids also discover the use and power of reading and writing.

Children will:
◆ understand that printed materials provide information.
◆ identify types of everyday print materials.
◆ recognize and use complete coherent sentences when speaking.

KNOW THESE WORDS!

There are certain important words to know that make reading faster and easier. When you see them, you need to be able to say them — quickly. Ask a grown-up to write the words on this page on index cards. Now use them to play games.

Words to Know!

I	go
am	to
like	here
a	is
we	my
see	at
can	dad
you	mom
the	look
and	love

FLASH CARDS

A grown-up places two words before you. She tells you what each one says. Can you point to and read each one? When you can read these two easily, add another. Add a word each day (or week or month) until you can read them all.

TAP IT!

To play this fast-paced game, use only the cards for the words you know. Place the cards before you. A grown-up calls out a word. Tap it if you see it. If you're right, it's yours. Can you pick up all the word cards this way?

SORT AND SAY

Have a grown-up make five cards for each word you are learning. Mix them up and lay them out before you. Pick up a word and say it. Line up the words that are the same.

MATCH, PAIRS, AND RECALL

A grown-up can make two sets of word cards. Use them to play the matching games on page 55.

SENTENCE STORIES

Once you know most of the words, a grown-up can lay the cards out with your special word cards in sentence stories for you to read:
I can go. We like to play. I love my mom. Look at my Stegasaurus.
Note the spaces between each word. Can you make your own sentence stories?

NOW I KNOW MY ABC'S

As you sing the letters in this well-known song, follow these steps …

Freeze! Don't move anything, except your eyes. Can you see letters? They're lurking on the cereal box, in magazines, on the computer. Point some out to a grown-up, and he'll tell you their names. Letters are amazing line shapes, and there are 26 different ones in the English alphabet. To put them together to form words, you've got to be able to tell one from the other. Celebrate each awesome letter of the alphabet with this alphabet circle dance!

"A, B, C, D, E, F, G

Circle moves to the right, then stops.

H, I, J, K, L, M, N, O, P
Circle moves to the left, then stops.

CLAP!!!

Q, R, S
Circle moves to the center. Kids raise hands and clap.

Continue the dance with the following steps

T, U, V (Kids lower hands while moving backward to edge of circle and clap.)
W, X (Circle moves to the center. Kids raise hands and clap.)
Y and Z (Kids lower hands while moving backward to edge of circle and clap.)
Now I've said my ABC's, (Circle moves to the right, then stops.)
Next time won't you sing with me?" (Circle moves to the left, then stops.)

26 FRIENDS FLASH CARDS

Imagine meeting 26 friends and having to remember all their names. That's what it's like learning the letters of the alphabet. It doesn't happen all at once. You get to know each one by spending time together. Say the name of each letter as you play with it in these many fun ways! Soon you'll know them all!

Here's what you do
....

1. A grown-up can write letters on half index cards as shown. Notice that there are two ways to write each letter, uppercase (A, B, C) and lowercase (a, b, c). Which kind starts your name? Which kind are the rest?

2. Set out an uppercase letter card you'd like to learn, like **T**. Point to the letter and say "Tee." Add a new letter each time you learn one. Set out the cards of the letters you've learned. Point to and say each letter name.

3. Don't go too fast — add a new card only when you're ready to meet a new letter!

4. When you've mastered the uppercase letters, you're ready to learn the lowercase letters the same way!

MoRe Fun for You!

THE CLAY WAY. Roll clay into thin logs. Use them to form the letters you're learning.

GIVE THEM A HAND! Can you think of a way to form each letter using the fingers of both hands? Take turns with a partner making letters and guessing them.

BIG BODY LETTERS. Can you make **c** with your body? How about a **t** or an **l**? You'll need another kid or two to help you with most of the rest! Try a **w** or **k.**

BENDABLES. A grown-up can cut heavy string or pipe cleaners into 2", 4", 6", and 8" (5, 10, 15, and 20 cm) lengths, leaving some whole. Store them in a zippered plastic bag. Use them to form letters. How would you form a **c** or an **s**? That's right; curve the pipe cleaners or the string!

EATING THE ALPHABET

Can eating letters help you remember their names? There's only one yummy way to find out — say the letter name before you eat each one!

Here's what you need

½ cup (125 ml) butter
   or margarine
1¼ cups (300 ml) flour
¼ cup (50 ml) sugar
Mixing spoon
Bowl
Foil
Cookie sheet
Spatula

Here's what you do

1. Blend the butter or margarine, flour, and sugar in the bowl.
2. Roll the dough into ropes. Form the dough into letters on a foil-covered cookie sheet.
3. With a grown-up's help, bake the letters at 300°F (150°C) for about 20 minutes.
4. Use the spatula to carefully lift the letters onto a plate and let them cool.

More Fun for You!

CEREAL SORT. Pour a handful of alphabet cereal on the table. Look for letters that are the same. Every time you find three, say their name and eat them!

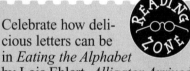

ALPHABET SOUP. Enjoy those oodles of noodles! Call out the names of the letters you see and know. Don't eat the letter that starts your name!

READING ZONE

Celebrate how delicious letters can be in *Eating the Alphabet* by Lois Ehlert, *Alligator Arrived with Apples: A Potluck Alphabet Feast* by Crescent Dragonwagon, and *ABC Yummy* by Lisa Jahn-Clough.

Teaching Time Vivid experiences enhance memory. So use the senses of touch and taste to increase learning! It's no small task to learn 52 letters (uppercase and lowercase). Children's love of food can help. Be on the lookout for alphabet foods: cookies, crackers, and pasta.

LETTER LOOK-OUT

Letters dwell almost everywhere.
Look around for letters you know.
Ask about the ones you'd like
to learn.

POINT IT OUT

Ask a grown-up to help you cut out a
shape like the one here. Tape one to
a pencil point or chopstick as shown.
Now use this cool gizmo to point out
letters all around. Walk through your
home or classroom pointing to letters
you know and calling out their
names.

TARGET LETTERS

Look at a newspaper or magazine
page. It's full of letters!
◆ Use your pointer to point out the
ones you know. Say their names.
◆ Search out a target letter, like **n.**
Use a highlighter to brighten all the
n's you see, both lowercase and
uppercase.

A A IS AN A IS A A

Although a letter might sometimes have a slightly different look, it's still the same letter. A Kmart **K,** for example, looks different from the **K** on a box of Kellogg's Special K, but it's still a **K.** People use different fonts, or letter styles, when they print. Ask a grown-up to show you all the fonts you can use on your computer. Wow!

COLLECT. Gather all sorts of letters in all sorts of fonts. Cut them from magazines. Print them from your computer and cut them out.

SORT. When you have a nice collection, spread them out on a table. Now sort your letters as you say their names: all **A's** in one pile, **B's** in another, and so on. Look at your piles and pick out your favorite fonts. Choose a letter and paste all its variations in size and design on a piece of paper.

SPELL. Look through the letter piles that contain the letters of your name. Pick out your favorite fonts. Paste the letters in order on a card. That's one fancy name!

Teaching Time

These activities tie letter learning to real life. Use everyday print as an opportunity to teach letter names. Point out letter names on the signs of stores you frequent, on the packaging of favorite foods, and in the titles of favorite books. Soon your child will be pointing them out to you!

MILK=CAP MANIA

Use milk caps to practice alphabet letter naming, sorting, and sequencing.

Here's what you need

52 plastic milk caps
Permanent marker

Here's what you do

Make the game:
A grown-up uses a marker to print an uppercase or lowercase letter clearly on the flat side of each cap.

Let's play!
1. First sort the letters into two piles: uppercase and lowercase. Set them up so you can see each letter.

2. Sing the ABC song as you search the pile for each uppercase letter, in the order of the song. Set the letters up in a line.

MATCH. Now look at the lowercase letters. Match each one to those in the line by placing it beneath its uppercase mate. If it's too hard to match the entire alphabet, match only the letters you've learned so far. The rest will soon become yours to use, so don't worry!

UP AND DOWN. Place all the milk caps in a bag. A grown-up reaches inside and pulls out a letter. If it's uppercase, stretch up on your tiptoes with your hands high in the air and shout, "uppercase!" If it's lowercase, squat down and whisper, "lowercase."

RECALL. Set out eight pairs of caps, face down, in rows of four. Follow the directions for Recall on page 55, only this time, match uppercase to lowercase letters.

ALPHAPET

Alphabet letters have a special order. Discover it as you make this critter!

Here's what you need

9 cardboard tubes
2½ yards (225 cm) yarn or string
Markers
Child safety scissors

Here's what you do

1. A grown-up cuts seven tubes into four parts each.

2. With grown-up help, cut the head and tail from the two whole tubes as shown. Attach the string as shown.

3. Use different colored markers to write the letters of the alphabet on each section. Print an uppercase letter on one side and a lowercase letter on the back.

4. Now, sing the alphabet song as you look for each letter and string the sections in order.

5. Knot the string around the tail section. Add a "leash" to the head as shown. Sing the alphabet song as you take your AlphaPet for a walk!

76 WOW! I'M READING!

MOre fun for you!

STEPPING STONES. Ask a grown-up to draw chalk stepping stones on the sidewalk or driveway and write a letter above each stepping stone. Sing the alphabet song as you hop from letter to letter.

A,B,C,D,E,F,G,H,I,J,K...

COMPUTER TIME. Ask a grown-up to set the computer with a large point size (about 36) and a bold font. Sing the alphabet song as you look for and type each letter. (If you need help, ask a grown-up to print each letter in uppercase letters on a strip of paper as you search). What kind of letters are printed on your keyboard? Uppercase or lowercase?

For alphabet fun with animals, try *Amazon Alphabet* by Martin and Tanis Jordan, *The Icky Bug Alphabet Book* by Jerry Pallotta, and *Animal Parade* by Jakki Wood.

Teaching Time

Sequence is part of life. A day has a beginning, middle, and end. So do stories. Words have first, next, and last parts. So do instructions. The letters of the alphabet have a special order, too, which most people learn through the alphabet song. Singing the song while looking at each letter is helpful for connecting the name to the symbol, and letters to a sequence.

ABCDEF GHIJKL MNOPQR STUVW XYZ

PHONICS FUN!

You know that each letter has a name — like **c** or **a** or **t**. Did you know that each letter also has a sound? Knowing the sounds is how you figure out what writing means.

cat

Here's how you do it:
Say the sound of each letter in this word: *cat*. Move your finger along from letter to letter as you say each sound. The trick is to blend the sounds together, one right after the next, for the letters you see: **c a t.**

Does that sound like a word to you? Sure it does — *cat!* Wow, you're reading!

Here are fun games to help you match letters with their sounds so you are reading words — just like that!

26 TERRIFIC LETTERS!

Knowing the sounds for every letter in the alphabet is a lot to learn. Celebrate a different letter each week with an action.

ACT THEM!

A grown-up holds up a letter card while you perform the matching action.

A ask (shrug shoulders)
B bounce
C clap
D dance
E exercise
F fly
G gallop

H hop
I inch (move finger like an inch-worm)
J jump
K kick
L look (shield eyes with hand)
M march
N no (use "no, no" finger gesture)
O open (motion with two hands)
P pat
Q quit (motion with two hands)

R run
S stop ("stop" hand gesture)
T tiptoe
U up (point upward)
V vacuum
W wave
X make X shape with both index fingers
Y yawn
Z zip (make motion of doing up a zipper)

MOrE FuN for YOu!

You can hear and see letters. Now, use your other senses to help you learn them.

EAT THEM! Place a letter card before you as you enjoy a snack that begins with the same sound. Here are some ideas to get you munching: apples, apricots, alphabet cereal for **A**; frosted flakes, French fries, or fruit salad for **F**; Quik (Nestle's), Quaker Oats for **Q**, and waffles, wontons, or water for **W**.

Here are more fun ways to experience letters and their sounds: *Alphabatics* by Suse MacDonald, *A You're Adorable* by Buddy Kaye, Fred Wise, and Sidney Lippman, and *Alison's Zinnia* by Anita Lobel.

Teaching Time

Letter symbols and sounds are abstract and very easy to confuse. Offering varied, multisensory experiences that link each letter to its sound and having the child practice them over a long period of time leads to mastery of the letter-sound match that's essential to reading.

STATE STANDARDS SAY...

Children will: match all consonant and short-vowel sounds to appropriate letters.

FEEL THEM! Start a "feely" letter collection. A grown-up can help you print the letter on cardboard and squeeze glue along its shape. As you say the letter's name, stick on stuff with an interesting texture that reminds you of its sound. How about beans for **b**? Or rice for **r**?

ALPHABET CROWNS

Make special crowns for your favorite letters of the alphabet (or the ones you're having trouble remembering). Decorate each one with letters and pictures of words that start with that letter sound.

Here's what you need

3" x 2" (7.5 x 60 cm) strip of
  construction paper
Thin markers
White paper
Scissors
Paste
Stapler

Here's what you do

1. Write the target letter all over the strip of paper (see Wild, Wacky Writing, page 102).

2. Think of three words that start with that letter. Draw them on the white paper. Cut around each picture and paste it to the center of the strip.

3. Ask a grown-up to place the strip around your head and staple it together so that it fits just right.

More Fun for You!

Here are some fun decorations to make your crowns extra special. Can you think of others?

A antennae (pipe cleaner and cotton balls)

B bag

C cat	**O** oval
D diamond	**P** pink pig
E elephant	**Q** quilt
F frog	**R** rainbow
G green grass	**S** star
H heart	**T** triangle
I inchworm	**U** up (an arrow)
J jet	**V** violet visor
K kite	**W** wave
L lightning bolt	**X** x-shape
M mouse	**Y** yellow band
N newspaper	**Z** zigzag edges

◆ For animal crowns, add ear shapes to the top and nose shapes or thin whiskers strips to the middle of the band.

◆ For shape crowns, cut out a large shape and paste it to the center of the band.

◆ For waves, grass, or zigzags, cut the top edge of the band.

READING ZONE

These books are full of ideas for Alphabet Crowns: *From Acorn to Zoo and Everything in Between in Alphabetical Order* by Satoshi Kitamura, *Flora McDonnell's ABC,* and *My First Dictionary* by Betty Root.

Teaching Time

Phonics is a system that links sounds to symbols. About 40 spoken sounds are matched with more than twice as many letters and spellings. This complex alphabetic code is learned over many years. It's challenging, but beginning readers start by learning the basic consonant and vowel sounds represented by the 26 letters.

Although some letters make several sounds, teach short sounds for the vowels at first. Later children can learn that each vowel also makes a long sound by saying its name.

◆ Roll up the bottom edge of a bag; fold a newspaper hat (see page 21); and cut a visor shape for these special crowns.

ALPHABET MATCHUPS

Hang things on a line! Hide stuff in a cabinet! Play games! Just be sure you've got an alphabet matchup!

LETTER LINEUP

Ask a grown-up to print the alphabet on wooden clothespins (one upper-case letter on each pin). Can you clip the letters onto a clothes-line in order?

◆ Search your home for fun letter-matching stuff to hang from each pin. How about a sock for **s,** a neck-lace for **n,** or a zipper for **z?** Keep hunting! Make your matches over time.

◆ Use your clothespins for flash-card matching. Draw (or cut and paste) pictures on to half index cards. Add these cards to the Alphabet Flash Cards on page 68. Now you can pair up:

Uppercase-letter clothespins with *uppercase*-letter cards

Uppercase-letter clothespins with *lowercase*-letter cards

Letter clothespins with same-sound pictures

TINY TREASURES

Ask a grown-up to glue two egg cartons together as shown. Paste letters to the center of each cup (combine **wx** and **yz**). You now have a special container for a collection of tiny treasures. As an ongoing activity, search for little items (or small magazine pictures) to match each letter. Remember, they must fit in the cups.

When your collection is complete, dump it out. Can you put each treasure back into its letter cup?

Teaching Time

Early, confident knowledge of the letter-sound relationship is a predictor of good reading comprehension in later years. Why? Because those who have it can rapidly decode (decipher) words. It's hard to understand what a sentence means when the reader has to struggle to figure out each word. Fluent reading makes sense; choppy reading does not!

Children will: match all consonant and short-vowel sounds to appropriate letters.

STATE STANDARDS SAY...

ELECTRONIC ALPHABETS

Plug them in ... turn them on. These flashy alphabets will keep you energized!

W IS FOR WEB

With a grown-up's help, search the Internet for "alphabet." You'll find amazing online picture dictionaries and interactive alphabet games!

ALPHABET ALBUM

On a computer, ask a grown-up to help you print a large (about 72 points) uppercase and lowercase letter in the top left corner of each page. Print out the 26 pages and assemble as an album (see page 110). Use clip art (from your computer), magazine pictures, or your own drawings to illustrate each letter page. Then, ask a grown-up to help you label each picture.

PHOTO FUN

Ask a grown-up to photograph you and your friends enjoying alphabet fun for each letter. You can eat an apple for the **a** photo, bounce a ball for the **b** photo, or pet your cat for the **c** photo. Have fun deciding what to do for each letter. Then, "click." Assemble photos in order in plastic sleeves and collect in a photo album. Write each letter on a small piece of paper and slide it into the corner of the sleeve.

TERRIFIC TAPES

Record family members, other kids, and yourself saying favorite words for each letter of the alphabet: "**A** is for astronaut, antennae, and asparagus!" Record kids and grown-ups singing the alphabet song or reading their favorite alphabet books.

FOCUS ON PHONICS

This handy viewer lets you focus on one letter — and its sound — at a time.

Here's what you need

Child safety scissors
Cardboard egg carton
Tape
Jumbo paper clips
White computer paper
Markers

Here's what you do

A grown-up makes the viewer:
1. Cut a two-cup section and its lid from the end of the egg carton.
2. Cut circles from the bottom of each section to make holes to look through.
3. Cut a 1" x 1½" (2.5 x 3.5 cm) window in the center of the lid for viewing the picture. (Note: The lid may already have a hole here.)
4. Seal shut with tape.
5. Slip jumbo paper clips onto either side of the window to hold the film.

You make the "film":
1. Ask a grown-up to cut a 1" x 11" (2.5 x 27.5 cm) strip of white paper with sections marked every 1½" (3.5 cm).
2. Write the target letter on the first square and draw words that start with that letter sound in the other squares.
3. Hold the viewer with the sealed end on top. Slide the film through the clips and in back of the window. Look through the eye holes toward the light. Enjoy the view as you say the letter sounds and name the items.

4

5

READING ZONE
Each of these tales focuses on a specific letter: *Wet World* by Norma Simon, *The Berenstains' B Book* by Stan and Jan Berenstain, and *Dinorella: A Prehistoric Fairy Tale* by Pamela Duncan Edwards.

Teaching Time

These activities are a good way to focus on any sounds a child is having trouble remembering. Challenge him to think of many words that start with the same letter sound. *Hand, horse, house,* and *heart* all start with the sound **h.** Link these words that start with the same letter sound to the letter symbols **H** and **h.**

MORe FUN foR YOU!

A LIBRARY OF LETTERS. Make a mini-book for each letter of the alphabet (follow the instructions for making a mini-book on page 108). Write the letter on each cover. On each page, draw a picture of something that starts with that letter sound. Ask a grown-up to help you label each picture.

WORD PUZZLERS

Just as puzzle pieces line up to form a picture, letters line up to form words! Fit these puzzle pieces together to build a word you can read all by yourself!

Here's what you need

Markers
4" x 6" (10 x 15 cm) index cards
Child safety scissors
Ziplock bag

Here's what you do

1. A grown-up can write a word from the list here on the bottom of each index card. You draw a picture of the word, or cut one out of a magazine and paste it on.
2. Make the puzzle by cutting between the letters.

3. Mix up the pieces in the bag. Can you put each puzzle together?
4. Now, ask a grown-up to help you read the word beneath the picture.

WORD PUZZLERS WORDS

Use consonant-vowel-consonant words such as: cat, fan, map, hen, pet, leg, pin, pig, six, pot, dog, top, sun, bug, pup.

MOre FuN foR YoU!

MAKE YOUR OWN WORD PUZZLERS.

Use family photos (mom, dad, cat, dog), pictures from magazines, or your own drawings. Be sure to have a grown-up write the word along the top or bottom of each puzzle.

READING ZONE

Beginning readers who enjoy figuring out puzzles with letter clues will love *Q is for Duck: An Alphabet Guessing Game* by Mary Elting and Michael Folsom, *Tomorrow's Alphabet* by George Shannon, and *Alphabet Riddles* by Susan Joyce.

Teaching Time

Here's what you say to guide the child through the exciting process of figuring out the word at the bottom of the picture:

1. "Watch and listen as I blend these sounds together to read a word. I put my finger under the first letter. I say and blend the sounds each letter makes as I move my finger to the next letter. I place my finger back at the beginning of the word, then sweep through as I say the word."

2. "Now, try it with me. Place your finger on top of mine and blend the sounds with me. Then sweep and say the word."

3. "Now use your finger to try it by yourself. Wow, you're really reading!"

STATE STANDARDS SAY...

Children will:
◆ match all consonant and short-vowel sounds to appropriate letters.
◆ be able to read simple one-syllable words and high-frequency words.

PHONICS GIZMOS

Ask a grown-up to make these word-building gizmos for you. Now you read the words you create!

FLIP BOOKS

On an index card, write the rime (see page 93) ending of a word family (like *-an*). Staple a stack of 1" x 2" (2.5 x 5 cm) onset (changing letter, see page 93) strips next to it as shown. Flip the letters to make words. For more fun, draw matching picture strips and staple them next to the word.

WORD WHEELS

On cereal-box cardboard, trace around an old CD twice and cut out two circles. Cut a ³⁄₄" x 1" (2 x 2.5 cm) window in one of the circles as shown. Connect the circles at the center with a paper fastener.*

Copy onsets and rimes onto the circles as shown.

Turn the wheel and read the words!

*Note: Paper fasteners pose a choking and poking danger to children. Adults should control the supply and insert them into the project.

WORD SLIDE

Cut two 2¹/₂" (6 cm) parallel slits in a large index card and write the rime of a word family to the right of it as shown. Cut a 1" x 11" (2.5 x 27.5 cm) strip of paper for the beginning letters and 1¹/₄" x 11" (3 x 27.5 cm) strip for drawings of the words. Pull the strips through the window and read the words. Match pictures to words. Make one for each of your favorite word families!

Teaching Time Use common rimes such as these for the Phonics Gizmos:

at, ap, an, ad, et, en, ed, it, ig, in, ip, ot, og, op, up, ug, un.

Skilled readers see patterns in words. What's known about a familiar word *(man)* can be quickly applied to help read an unknown word *(can)*. In these activities, children focus on the reliable rime (chunk of the syllable that includes the vowel and following letters — *an*) and blend it with the changing onset (the part of the syllable that comes before the vowel — *c, m, t, pl,* and so on). Teaching words by rime family is very effective because after children learn a few dozen rimes, they can read hundreds of words. And yes, these words do *rhyme!*

Children will: understand that as letters of words change, so do the sounds. **STATE STANDARDS SAY...**

BUILDING WORDS

Change a letter, change a word. That's how our alphabet works! Awesome, isn't it?

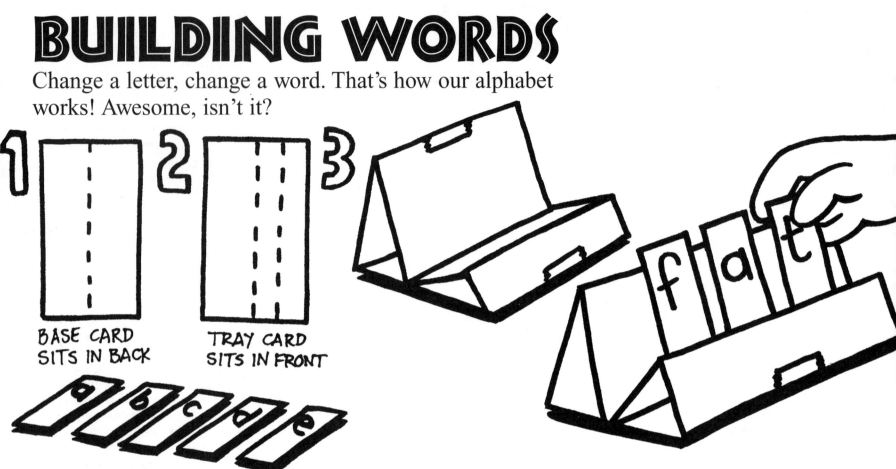

1 BASE CARD SITS IN BACK

2 TRAY CARD SITS IN FRONT

3

Here's what you need

Tape

Two 4" x 6" (10 x 15 cm) index cards

Child safety Scissors

3" x 5" (7.5 x 12.5 cm) index cards

Black permanent marker

Here's what you do

A grown-up makes the word-building tray:

1. Fold and tape the two large index cards as shown.

2. Cut the small index cards into four pieces. Print a lower-case letter at the top of each one. These are the letter cards for word building.

You build the words!

Set out the tray and a few letters. A grown-up will help you break apart a word like *fat*. What's the first sound you hear? **f.** What letter makes that sound? **f!** Set the **f** card on the tray. Keep listening for sounds and looking for letters. Set them in the tray to spell *fat*!

You take the challenge!

Change:

- ◆ fat to mat
- ◆ fat to fast
- ◆ mat to man to can to cat
- ◆ cat to cot to cut

Find little words from the letters of a bigger word:

- ◆ fast (fat, sat, fast)
- ◆ spend (send, end, den, pen, Ned)
- ◆ stop (pot, spot, top, pots)
- ◆ scrub (cub, rub, sub, cubs, rubs, bus, us)

MORE FUN FOR YOU!

ALIEN TALK. You can build "alien talk" words, too. These silly words are just nonsense. It's fun to figure out how they would be spelled: *zef, mox, neb, jit, cag, vud.*

MYSTERY SENTENCES. A grown-up can write mystery sentences for you to figure out. You now know enough about letters and words to really read these sentences! To figure out each word, have a grown-up guide you as described on page 91.

A cat can nap.
A bad rat sat.
A dog jogs on a log.
A bug is snug on a rug.
A pig can jig.
A dog and a cat hug.

READING ZONE For word-building practice, read *Andy: That's My Name* by Tomie dePaola or *Word Wizard* by Cathryn Falwell.

Change a letter, change a word is a simple yet powerful concept that gives kids control of the alphabetic principle.

Phonemic awareness activities give children the understanding that spoken language sound units can be manipulated. By linking these sounds to letter symbols, children make a learning leap and manipulate letters to create new written words. Kids are then empowered with a means not only to unlock meaning from print, but to read and put their own ideas into print as well. To help a child figure out the new words, guide him as described on page 91.

STATE STANDARDS SAY... Children will:

- ◆ associate spoken sounds with the letters that represent them.
- ◆ spell independently using sounds of the alphabet and knowledge of letter names.
- ◆ understand that as letters of words change, so do the sounds.
- ◆ begin to use this knowledge to read words and simple stories.

WRITE ON!

Create a birthday card for your brother. Make a menu for your Pizza Kitchen. You're writing! When you write, you share your special ideas. You can make someone very happy with an "I love you" message. You can tell about a day at the lake and send your story to Grandma, far away. You can add foods you like to the shopping list so Dad remembers to buy them. Whether you share the fun or report the facts, writing is useful. So, grab a pencil, and let's start writing!

MY OFFICE

It's so much fun to write — especially in your own office.

Here's what you need

Any or all of the following:
Pads of paper
Sheets of blank and lined paper
Stationery
Envelopes (you can use ones
    recycled from junk mail)
Pencils: Colored and plain
Pens: All sorts, including markers
    and ballpoints
Index cards
Child safety scissors
Alphabet stencils
Rubber stamps
Gummed stamps and labels
Stapler
Tape
Glue stick
Paper clips

Here's what you do

The best spot for your office is at a
kid-sized desk or on a small table.
If there's a bulletin board nearby,
post a calendar, important reminders,
and your wonderful writing and
drawing. It's great if a grown-up
lets you also use a computer for
making messages.

MORE FUN FOR YOU!

OFFICE SIGNS. Create signs on construction paper or make a handy door hanger. Your signs might say: Open, Closed, Executive Director, Will Return, and Come In.

BUSINESS CARDS. Cut index cards in half and write your name and phone number on each one. Draw a logo (a design that says something special about you) on each card.

STATIONERY. Draw a special design at the top of a sheet of white paper with a black marker. Ask a grown-up to make you several sheets on a photocopier.

IT'S IN THE MAIL

Send some mail. Get some back. Mail is how we exchange important messages with people both near and far.

Here's what you need

Small paper bag
Marking pens
Scissors
Strong tape

Here's what you do

Make a mailbox:
1. Fold the bag back about 3" (7.5 cm) from the top. Here's your space to write your name and decorate the bag.
2. Have a grown-up snip down the sides as shown and tuck the top part into the bag.

3. Use strong tape to hang the mailbox on your bedroom door.
   Be sure everyone in your family makes a mailbox so you can all exchange messages!

More Fun for You!

YOU'VE GOT MAIL! Any sort of writing you seal in an envelope makes a letter. Make any of the mail on this page. You may want to try the grown-up way using words like *Dear* or *To* and *From*. Deliver it to that person's mailbox. If you want to write to friends or family members who live far away, ask a grown-up to help you use the postal system. Either way, you're sure to get mail back addressed to you!

POSTCARDS. On one side of a large index card, draw a picture or paste on a magazine photo. Write on the back as shown, with a short message on the left side and the address on the right.

GREETING CARDS. Fold a sheet of paper to make a card. It's that simple! Usually a greeting card has a picture on the front and a special message inside. You can send cards on special days like birthdays or holidays. Or, send a card anytime to say "Thank You" or "I Love You."

Mom and I flew this kite at the beach.

Nick Chu
37 17ᵀᴴ St.
Los Angeles
CA 98049

WILD, WACKY WRITING

Fifty-two letters (uppercase and lowercase) are a lot to learn. Writing them in wacky ways is a fun way to remember them. As you form each letter, say its name and the sound it makes.

A Print A's on accordion-folded paper or ads.

B Print blue, brown, and black B's on bags.

C Print C's on cardboard or comics.

D Print D's on doilies.

E Print E's on egg-carton lids.

F Print F's on folded paper.

G Print green or gray G's on green or gray paper.

H Trace around your hand. Fill the hand shape with H's.

I Print I's with ink on ice-cream cartons.

J Form J's in the margins of junk mail.

K Print K's on Kleenex.

L Print L's on lids.

M Print M's with markers on magazines.

N Print N's on newspaper.

O Print O's on O-shaped paper.

P Print purple and pink P's on paper plates.

Q Print Q's with Q-Tips dipped in paint.

R Print red R's on ripped paper.

S Print S's on Styrofoam trays.

T Print T's on torn paper towels.

U Print U's while under an umbrella.

V Print violet V's.

W Print W's with watercolors on white, wet paper.

X Print X's on X-shaped paper.

Y Print yellow Y's or print on yellow paper.

Z Print Z's on paper cut in a zigzag.

SPELL=A=PHONE

This phone tells you how to spell words! Use it to listen for letter sounds. Link the sounds to the letter symbols. Jot down the letter. That's how you spell. Presto, you've written a word!

You listen for sounds!
Hold the phone up to your ear and segment a word into the mouthpiece: **p i g.** What sounds do you hear? What letter represents each sound? Write each letter in the same order in which you hear the sounds. Hey, you just wrote a word!

Here's what you need
. . . .

Child safety scissors
4 cardboard tubes
Masking tape

Here's what you do
. . . .

You and a grown-up make the phone:

1. Cut the tubes into segments as shown.

2. Fit them together with masking tape so that one end goes up to the child's ear and the other is near her mouth.

MOre FUn fOr yOu!

JOT DOWN A JOURNAL. Write one or more Print Pal sentences each day at the top of a sheet of white paper. Illustrate your story with crayons or markers. Keep all pages together in an album (page 110).

SNIP A SENTENCE. A grown-up cuts apart the words of a sentence and mixes them up. Can you lay them out in order? Store words in a zippered plastic bag for more put-together practice.

Teaching Time

Being Print Pals is the ideal way to share with a child how writing works. Develop literacy awareness with on-the-spot lessons such as:
◆ As you add the **e** to lake, explain how it makes the **a** say its name while the **e** itself is silent.
◆ Explain how one can't really figure out the sounds in *the.* It's just one of those common words you remember how to spell and say.
◆ Show how to create spaces between words by marking them with two fingers.
◆ Explain how a sentence starts with an uppercase word and ends with a period.
    Whatever you do automatically, share aloud with the child.

STATE STANDARDS SAY...

Children will:
◆ write by moving from left to right and from top to bottom.
◆ use letters and phonetically spelled words to write about experiences, stories, people, and events.

BOOKS GALORE

Anyone can make a book! Just bind some pages between covers with staples or string. Now fill those pages with your own words and pictures. Presto, you've got a book!

LITTLE LIBRARY BOOKS

Fold a sheet of paper in half. Cut along the fold. Hold the two pieces together and fold them in half. Staple them together along the fold. Be sure to write the title and the author (that's you!) on the front cover. *Little Library Books* are perfect for:

LETTERS. Focus on one letter, say **L**. So, the title is *The L Book*. On each page, draw a picture and write a label for a word that starts with **L** *(ladybug, lollipop, lips, love …).*

WORD FAMILIES. The title is *The -at Book*. On each page, draw a picture and write a word that rhymes with -at *(mat, rat, bat, fat …).*

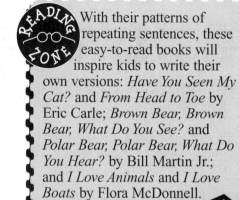

CATEGORIES. Each page of these books shows a word and a picture of things that are alike in some way. *The Red Book* shows an apple, a fire engine, a stop sign. *The Farm Book* shows a pig, a cow, a tractor. *The Friend Book* shows each of your friends on a page.

AWESOME ALBUMS

To make an album, stack several sheets of blank paper. Use construction or stiff paper for the front cover. Punch three or four holes along the left edge. Connect with paper fasteners* or string. Awesome albums are perfect for:

Jason can sing.

Margaret can build.

*Note: Paper fasteners pose a choking and poking danger to children. Adults should control the supply and insert them into the project.

JOURNALS. Collect daily writing in an album. The writing can be your own, Print Pal writing (page 106), or Language Experience Stories (pages 26-27).

SCRAPBOOKS. Keep a scrapbook of a family trip or other special event. Paste souvenirs like tickets, postcards, or brochures onto the pages and label each one. Add your own drawings and favorite memories.

YOU AND ME BOOKS. Write this book with a friend. On one page, write something about you. On the facing page, your friend writes something about himself. Your book might be like this:
Margaret likes oranges.
Jason likes bananas.
Margaret can build.
Jason can sing.
Margaret is 4.
Jason is 5.

ACCORDION BOOKS

Accordion books can be made in any size or length. For a basic book, cut an 8½" x 11" (21.25 x 27.5 cm) sheet of paper in half the long way. Tape the two strips together. Accordion-fold into eight sections. Paste an index card to the first and last sections. Slip a length of thin ribbon between the card and the paper at each end as shown. When the book is closed, wrap the ribbon around the covers and tie in a bow.

Accordion books are just right for:
ALPHABET. Write a letter and draw a matching picture in each section for each letter of the alphabet.
RETELLING. Retell a tale by drawing and labeling an event from your favorite story in each section (see storyboard, page 19).
SEQUENCE. Use each section to show events in order: from seed to tree, from baby to you, from egg to frog.

Teaching Time

Because learning to read and learning to write are so interrelated and mutually reinforcing, they must happen at the same time. Children need ample opportunities to express themselves on paper. A wide variety of simple, blank books, such as these, encourages imaginative writing. Remember, writing is all attempts to communicate in print. Scribbling, labeling, invented spelling, and your recordings of a child's words are all exciting forms of written communication that empower the child with authorship!

STATE STANDARDS SAY...

Children will: use letters and phonetically spelled words to write about experiences, stories, people, and events.

WRITING TO READ!

Where can you find a book you can really read? Write it yourself!

Here's what you need

Paper
Scissors
Stapler
Markers

Here's what you do

1. Make several Little Library Books (page 108). You or a grown-up can write stories like the ones shown here in each one. Write one sentence on each page.

2. Combine words you can read by blending sounds (page 91) with Words to Know (page 64). Draw pictures on each page. Point to each word with your finger. Say the word or say the letter sounds to figure it out. *Wow, you're reading!*

I Can

I can run.
I can skip.
I can hop.
I can jump.
I can go.
I can stop.

I Am

I am Blake.
I am Mom.
I am Dad.
I am a dog.
I am a cat.
I am a rat.

I See

I see the sun.
I see the top.
I see the hog.
I see the bug.
I see the van.
I see the box.

READING ZONE

I Love You: A Rebus Poem by Jean Marzollo, features phonetically spelled, high-frequency words for first reading success.

Teaching Time

Research shows that successful readers rely on the text, not pictures or context, to figure out words. Emergent readers develop this important strategy when given text they can sound out successfully. Although sentences such as "Dan can fan a fat cat" sound contrived to us, they are intriguing to beginning readers. The purpose of decodable text is to provide practice in phonics skills, not to present great literature. Offering children text they can master builds the self-concept, "I am a reader. I am a writer." Fill books with sentences such as these that focus on a particular short vowel.

A: A cat can nap.
E: Ned met a red hen.
I: A pig jigs in a pit.
O: Hot rods stop on mops
U: A bug on a rug is snug.

STATE STANDARDS SAY...

Children will:
◆ read simple one-syllable and high-frequency words.
◆ write consonant-vowel-consonant words.

BEYOND THE TALE

A book can take you on a wondrous journey. You can learn exciting new facts about your favorite animal or find out how to bake a new kind of delicious cookie. You can stroll through the woods with Little Red Riding Hood or chase after the Gingerbread Man on the back of the wolf.

And reading the book is just the beginning of the adventure! With these fun activities, you can make your favorite stories come alive. You can explore, answer questions, and discover. So let's read on!

IT'S A FACT!

Want to learn about volcanoes, pets, or the weather? It's easy! All you have to do is read nonfiction, or fact, books — they're filled with exciting information.

LAVA

METEOR

pyramid

WORDS, WORDS, WORDS

1. Ask a grown-up to preview a nonfiction book for you and pick out a few interesting words: lava, antennae, gravity, meteor, evergreen, pyramid, freedom

2. They're cool-sounding, aren't they? Guess what each word might mean.

3. As you read the book together, listen for these words. Do you want to change your guess?

4. Talk with the grown-up about what the words really mean.

5. Use your new words when you talk about what you learned.

EENY-TINY THEATER

an turn any favorite tale into a puppet show. Just transform
ue box into a little stage. Then let the play begin!

Here's what you need

tissue box
paper
s
ards
afety scissors

g straws

Here's what you do

Make the stage:
A grown-up can help you cut the box as shown.

Make the backdrop:
How many different settings are in the story? A setting is the place where a part of the story happens. You can show each setting by making a backdrop for your stage.
1. Fold the white paper as shown so that it hangs down along the back of the stage.
2. Use markers to draw the setting. For "Goldilocks and the Three Bears," you'll need to make backdrops for the outside of the bears' cottage, and rooms with bowls, chairs, and beds.

Make the puppets:
How many different characters are in

I KNOW! I WANT TO KNOW!

Before you open a nonfiction book, take a few moments to think about what you already know about the topic. As you read the book and look at the pictures with a grown-up, you can talk about:

WHAT YOU KNOW
◆ Oh, I see …
◆ Wow, it's awesome that …
◆ That's just like …
◆ The most important thing about _____ is …

WHAT YOU WANT TO KNOW
◆ Who … ? Where … ? Why… ? What … ? How … ?
◆ What if … ?
◆ What about … ?
◆ I wonder . . . ?
◆ I want to know more about …
Read on to discover the answers to your questions.

DO IT YOURSELF!

An activity book is a special kind of nonfiction book full of fun things to make and do. Ask a grown-up to help you read the instructions aloud. Follow them together. Hey, you've baked a cookie, made a hat, or folded an awesome paper airplane. And reading made it happen!

DAZZLING DIAGRAMS

Make a diagram (a labeled picture of something from the book). For example, after reading a book about trees, draw one! Label the trunk, branches, roots, bark, and leaves with words and arrows. Or, draw an insect and label its thorax, abdomen, head, and legs.

leaves

branches

bark

trunk

roots

MORE FUN FOR YOU!

◆ Make the sequence crown on page 18 and use the squares to tell a science story.

◆ Instead of letters, fill the headband on page 18 with pictures and words about your topic.

◆ Make the Wordwear necklace on page 56. Use the large card to state the topic and the smaller cards to state facts.

◆ Choose a book to make on pages 108-111. Fill it with pictures and facts about your topic.

WONDER WEBS

Did you just read a book about frogs? Draw a frog and write the word frog in the center of a sheet of paper. Draw a circle around it. Draw several lines coming out from the circle as shown. At the end of each one, write a word or short phrase that tells about the frog.

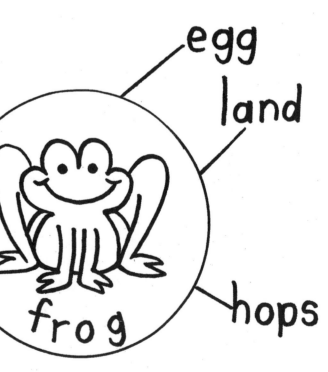

egg

land

tadpole

swims

water

hops

frog

◆ Invite friends to be puppeteers or to watch the show.

◆ Add tickets and programs (Let's Pretend with Print, page 62).

READING ZONE

Enjoy the classic tale *The Three Bears,* as retold by Paul Galdone. Then, compare these clever versions: *Somebody and the Three Blairs* by Marilyn Tolhurst, *The Three Little Javelinas* by Susan Lowell, and *Deep in the Forest* by Brinton Turkle.

Teaching Time

The best comprehension test is to have children retell what you've read aloud to them. Making a puppet show is an authentic and enjoyable way. Children clearly learn the terms "setting" and "character" as they hold the puppets and place backdrops on the stage.

STATE STANDARDS SAY...

Children will:
- ◆ retell familiar stories.
- ◆ identify characters, settings, and events of the story.
- ◆ know simple story structure.

---

the story? Characters, the people or critters the story is about, are the stars of the show! You'll need to make Goldilocks, Papa Bear, Mama Bear, and Baby Bear.

1. Draw each character on half of an index card.

2. Cut out the puppets and tape a straw to the back of each one as shown.

It's Showtime!

Retell the tale of "Goldilocks and the Three Bears" as if your audience has never heard it before.

1. Show the events of the story in order. Change the backdrop to match the scene.

2. Hold the top of the straw to place the puppets in front of the backdrop. Use different voices for each character.

STORYBOOK COOK

What's cooking on the stove? Mmm, it smells like gingerbread! Or maybe it's porridge. Only those who help you bake it can help you eat it!

Here's what you need

¼ cup (50 ml) oil
¼ cup (50 ml) honey
¾ cup (175 ml) milk
1 egg
2½ cups (625 ml) flour
2 teaspoons (10 ml) baking powder
½ teaspoon (2 ml) baking soda
½ teaspoon (2 ml) salt

Here's what you do

Who will help me beat the wet ingredients?
Put the oil, honey, milk, and egg into a mixing bowl. Use an egg beater to mix them together.

Who will help me mix the dry ingredients?
In another bowl, stir together the flour, baking powder, baking soda, and salt.

Who will help me add the dry ingredients to the wet?
Stir as you add until completely blended.

Who will help me bake the bread?
Pour into a well-greased 9" x 5" (22.5 x 12.5 cm) loaf pan. Bake in a 325°F (160°C) oven for one hour. Bread is done when brown and a toothpick comes out clean from the middle. Remove from pan and cool on a rack.

Who will help me eat the bread?
Yum! It's delicious to share, buttered or toasted, with friends the next day.

These tasty tales all include food: *The Gingerbread Man* by Eric A. Kimmel, *Hansel and Gretel,* as retold by Jane Ray, and *Stone Soup* by Marcia Brown.

Invite the child to retell the tale as you cook together. Encourage him to recall the characters and setting or to act out the part of a favorite character.

Teaching Time

ON WITH THE SHOW!

An interview with the Big Bad Wolf! A bug expert with her collection! Someone selling a new kind of spinning wheel that turns straw into gold! The only way to see TV shows this exciting is to create them yourself!

INTERESTING INTERVIEWS

Have a friend play the part of a favorite storybook character and use the mike shown here to interview her. Then, switch characters.

Let's say the characters from "The Three Billy Goats Gruff," "Little Red Riding Hood," and "The Three Little Pigs" are on your show. You might ask ...

◆ the Troll: Why didn't you catch any goats for dinner?

◆ the Little Pigs one and two: What building material might you try next time?

◆ the two Wolves (one from each tale): How are you guys alike? How are you different?

How could you trick the wolf next time?

CRAZY COMMERCIALS

Sell a product from a favorite story. Here are some ideas:

◆ A house made of gingerbread
◆ Pig's brick house
◆ Cinderella's glass slippers
◆ Shoes made by elves in the night
◆ A spinning wheel that turns straw into gold

See how many good things you can think to say about each product to make your audience want to buy it!

BE AN EXPERT!

You've read that book about bugs. Now you're an expert! Tell all you know about bugs to your television audience. Make your report exciting by showing pictures you've drawn or live bugs you've captured for the day. (Then, return them to their homes.)

If bugs aren't your specialty, your dog or cat would be pleased to appear while you report on pets. You could share your rock collection. Or, tell what you know about how to make friends.

HUFF-AND-PUFF SCIENCE

Be a huff-and-puff scientist. Do you and the Big Bad Wolf get the same results?

Here's what you need

Dried grass or straw
Twigs
Lego-type blocks
Jumbo fast-food drinking straw

Here's what you do

1. Make three small "houses" (clumps): one of straw, one of twigs, one of blocks.

2. What do you predict will happen when you use the drinking straw to blow hard at each house. Now try it! What really happens?

3. Could a pig build a house? Could a wolf blow it down? Can air move things?

READING ZONE

Read a fresh version of *The Three Little Pigs* by Marie-Louise Gay or Margot Zemach. Then try your own air experiments with *Science Play!* by Jill Frankel Hauser and *Air & Flying* by David Evans and Claudette Williams.

Enjoy learning more about the world with *Planting a Rainbow* by Lois Ehlert, *My Hen is Dancing* by Karen Wallace, and *I'm a Caterpillar* by Jean Marzollo.

Teaching Time

Stories, as well as your child's natural curiosity about things like water, stars, bugs, and animals, can elicit questions that are the perfect springboard to reading nonfiction text. Present fact books as an exciting way to learn more, answer questions, and explore.

STATE STANDARDS SAY...

Children will: listen to and respond to a wide variety of literature, including nonfiction and informational material.

MORe FUN fOr YOU!

As you — and the Big Bad Wolf — know, air can be mighty powerful. Try this experiment for more huff-and-puff fun.

1. Collect all sorts of objects (paper, feather, block, leaf, stick …).

2. Set them on the ground in a line.

3. Predict which one will travel farthest with just one puff of air through a drinking straw.

4. Now, use your straw and your breath to find out.

LETTER CHART

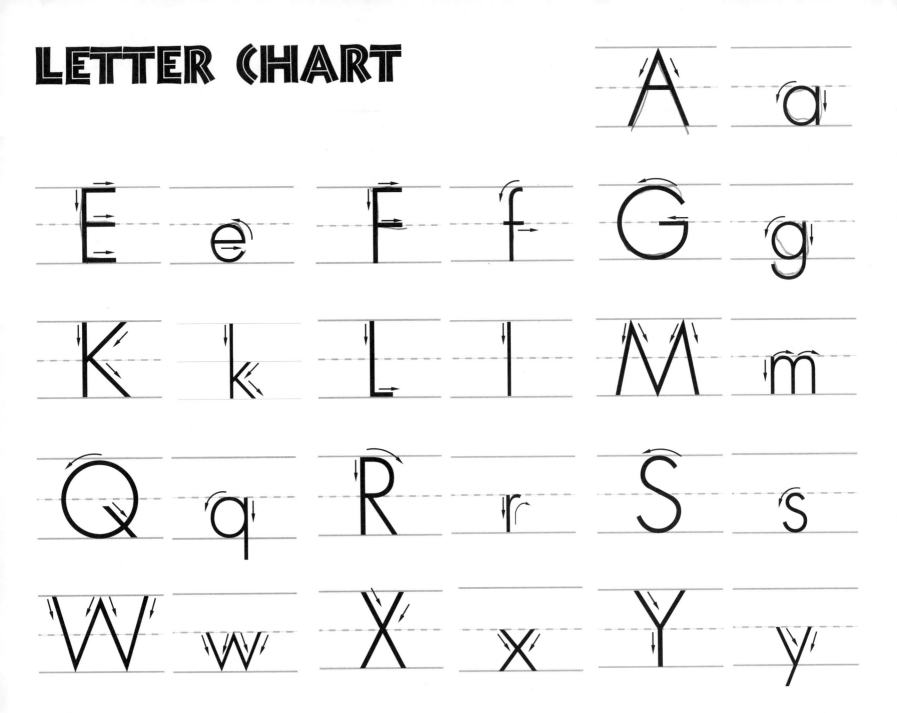

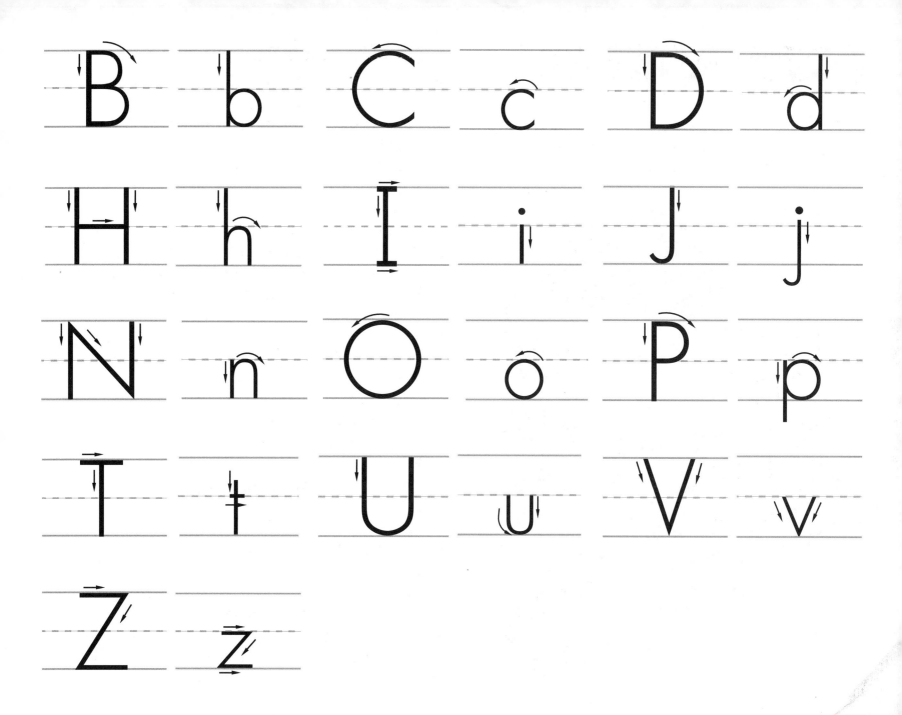

ALPHABET LISTS

Here are some additional ideas for interactive letter cards:

LETTER CARDS

As the child forms each letter, she says its name and the sound it makes.

A Print A's on accordion-folded paper or ads.
B Print blue, brown, and black B's on bags.
C Print C's on cardboard or comics.
D Print D's on doilies.
E Print E's on egg carton lids.
F Print F's on folded paper.
G Print green and gray G's on green or gray paper.
H Trace around your hand. Fill the hand shape with H's.
I Print I's with ink on ice cream cartons.
J Form J's in the margins of junk mail.
K Print K's on Kleenex.
L Print L's on lids.
M Print M's with markers on magazines.
N Print N's on newspaper.
O Print O's on O-shaped paper.
P Print purple and pink P's on paper plates.
Q Print Q's with watercolor-dipped Q-Tips.
R Print red R's on ripped paper.
S Print S's on styrofoam trays.
T Print T's on torn towels.
U Print U's while under the table.
V Print violet V's.
W Print W's with watercolor on white, wet paper.
X Print X's on X-shaped paper.
Y Print yellow Y's or print on yellow pages.
Z Print Z's on zig-zag paper (edges cut with pinking shears).

FOOD LETTER CARDS

The child tastes and smells each matching snack as he looks at the letter and says its sound.

A apples, apricots, alphabet cereal
B banana, burritos, bagels
C carrots, cookies, cake, crackers
D donuts, dates, dip
E egg drop soup, eggplant, English muffins
F frosted flakes, French fries, fruit salad
G grapes, graham crackers, garlic bread
H hot dogs, honey, hot chocolate
I ice cream, Italian bread, instant pudding
J jam, juice, Jell-O
K kiwi, Kool Aid, kidney beans
L lemonade, lime sherbet, lettuce
M muffin, m&m's, milk, marshmallows
N noodles, nectarines, nuts
O oatmeal cookies, onion bagels, olives
P popcorn, peanut butter, pickles
Q Quik (Nestle's), Quaker Oats, quince jelly
R raisins, Rice Crispies, radish
S sandwiches, soup, spaghetti
T toast, tacos, tofu
U upside-down cake
V vanilla ice cream, Velveta cheese
W waffles, won tons, water
X Kix, box lunch
Y yogurt, yams
Z zucchini, zoo cookies, Zwieback biscuits

ACTION LETTER CARDS

You hold up a letter card while the child performs the matching action.

A ask (shrug shoulders)
B bounce
C clap
D disco dance
E exercise
F fly
G gallop
H hop
I inch (make finger look like inch worm)
J jump
K kick
L look (hand above eyes)
M march
N no (use "no, no" finger gesture)
O open (motion with two hands)
P pat
Q quit (motion with two hands)
R run
S stop ("stop" hand gesture)
T tiptoe
U up (point upward)
V vacuum
W wave
X make "x" shape with both index fingers
Y yawn
Z zip (make zipping motion with hands)

"FEELY" LETTER COLLECTION

You print the letter on cardboard and squeeze white glue along its shape. The child can stick interesting-feeling materials to the letter as she says its name and sound.

A accordion-fold strips; acorns

B beans

C coffee grinds, cornmeal

D dots

E egg shells; erasers

F feathers, bits of foil

G glue (heap it on, but don't stick anything in it)l glitter

H holes

I icing; insects (toy)

J jelly beans

K Kix; keys

L leaves, letters (alphabet cereal)

M macaroni

N newspaper (small torn pieces); nuts

O oatmeal; orzo (pasta)

P pipe cleaners

Q quick oats; Q-tips

R rice; rubber bands

S sand, sugar, salt

T tea (break apart a tea bag); twist-tie

U umbrellas (small decorative paper ones)

V velvet; Velcro

W wax rubbed from a candle

X Kix; Trix

Y yarn

Z zigzag (a grown-up can give you strips of construction paper cut on both sides with pinking shears)

INDEX

W

MORE GOOD BOOKS FROM WILLIAMSON PUBLISHING

Williamson books are available from your bookseller or directly from Williamson Publishing. Please see last page for ordering information or to visit our website.
Thank you.

WILLIAMSON'S *LITTLE HANDS*® BOOKS...

SETTING THE STAGE FOR LEARNING

* BUILD EARLY LEARNING SKILLS
* SUPPORT ALL LEARNING STYLES
* PROMOTE SELF-ESTEEM

THE FOLLOWING *LITTLE HANDS*® BOOKS FOR AGES 2 TO 6 ARE EACH 144 PAGES, FULLY ILLUSTRATED, TRADE PAPER, 10 X 8, $12.95 US.

AROUND-THE-WORLD ART & ACTIVITIES
VISITING THE 7 CONTINENTS THROUGH CRAFT FUN
BY JUDY PRESS

LITTLE HANDS PAPER PLATE CRAFTS
CREATIVE ART FUN FOR 3- TO 7-YEAR-OLDS
BY LAURA CHECK

ARTSTARTS FOR LITTLE HANDS!
FUN DISCOVERIES FOR 3- TO 7-YEAR-OLDS
BY JUDY PRESS

THE LITTLE HANDS PLAYTIME! BOOK
50 ACTIVITIES TO ENCOURAGE COOPERATION & SHARING
BY REGINA CURTIS

PARENT'S GUIDE CHILDREN'S MEDIA AWARD
ALPHABET ART
WITH A TO Z ANIMAL ART & FINGERPLAYS
BY JUDY PRESS

AMERICAN BOOKSELLER PICK OF THE LISTS
RAINY DAY PLAY!
EXPLORE, CREATE, DISCOVER, PRETEND
BY NANCY FUSCO CASTALDO

PARENTS' CHOICE GOLD AWARD
CHILDREN'S BOOK-OF-THE-MONTH CLUB SELECTION
FUN WITH MY 5 SENSES
ACTIVITIES TO BUILD LEARNING READINESS
BY SARAH A. WILLIAMSON

REAL LIFE AWARD
CHILDREN'S BOOK-OF-THE-MONTH CLUB MAIN SELECTION
THE LITTLE HANDS ART BOOK
EXPLORING ARTS & CRAFTS WITH 2- TO 6-YEAR-OLDS
BY JUDY PRESS

EARLY CHILDHOOD NEWS DIRECTORS' CHOICE AWARD
PARENTS' CHOICE APPROVED
SHAPES, SIZES & MORE SURPRISES!
A LITTLE HANDS EARLY LEARNING BOOK
BY MARY TOMCZYK

PARENTS' CHOICE APPROVED
THE LITTLE HANDS BIG FUN CRAFT BOOK
CREATIVE FUN FOR 2- TO 6-YEAR-OLDS
BY JUDY PRESS

PARENTS' CHOICE APPROVED
THE LITTLE HANDS NATURE BOOK
EARTH, SKY, CRITTERS & MORE
BY NANCY FUSCO CASTALDO

MATH PLAY!
80 WAYS TO COUNT & LEARN
BY DIANE MCGOWAN & MARK SCHROOTEN

WILLIAMSON'S KIDS CAN!® BOOKS...

WHERE ALL KIDS CAN SOAR!

* ENCOURAGE QUESTIONING AND SELF-EXPRESSION
* LEARNING EXPERIENCES TO GROW WITH
* KIDS DIG THEM!

THE FOLLOWING *KIDS CAN!*® BOOKS FOR AGES 5 TO 13 ARE EACH 144 TO 178 PAGES, FULLY ILLUS-TRATED, TRADE PAPER, 11 X 8½, $12.95 US.

WILLIAMSON'S *KIDS CAN!*® BOOKS

ART & CRAFTS

PARENTS' CHOICE GOLD AWARD
AMERICAN BOOKSELLER PICK OF THE LISTS
OPPENHEIM TOY PORTFOLIO BEST BOOK AWARD

THE KIDS' MULTICULTURAL ART BOOK

ART & CRAFT EXPERIENCES FROM AROUND THE WORLD

BY ALEXANDRA M. TERZIAN

TEACHERS' CHOICE AWARD
PARENT'S GUIDE CHILDREN'S MEDIA AWARD
DR. TOY BEST VACATION PRODUCT

CUT-PAPER PLAY!

DAZZLING CREATIONS FROM CONSTRUCTION PAPER

BY SANDI HENRY

AMERICAN BOOKSELLER PICK OF THE LISTS
OPPENHEIM TOY PORTFOLIO BEST BOOK AWARD
SKIPPING STONES NATURE & ECOLOGY HONOR AWARD

ECOART!

EARTH-FRIENDLY ART & CRAFT EXPERIENCES FOR 3- TO 9-YEAR-OLDS

BY LAURIE CARLSON

EARLY CHILDHOOD NEWS DIRECTORS' CHOICE AWARD
REAL LIFE AWARD

VROOM! VROOM!

MAKING 'DOZERS, 'COPTERS, TRUCKS & MORE

BY JUDY PRESS

WILLIAMSON'S *KIDS CAN!*® BOOKS

SCIENCE

THE KIDS' BOOK OF WEATHER FORECASTING

BUILD A WEATHER STATION, "READ" THE SKY & MAKE PREDICTIONS!

WITH METEOROLOGIST MARK BREEN & KATHLEEN FRIESTAD

MORE WILLIAMSON BOOKS BY JILL FRANKEL HAUSER!

AMERICAN BOOKSELLER PICK OF THE LISTS
DR. TOY BEST VACATION PRODUCT

KIDS' CRAZY ART CONCOCTIONS

50 MYSTERIOUS MIXTURES FOR ART & CRAFT FUN
AGES 6–12, 160 PAGES, $12.95

AMERICAN BOOKSELLER PICK OF THE LISTS
PARENTS' CHOICE HONOR AWARD

GIZMOS & GADGETS

CREATING SCIENCE CONTRAPTIONS THAT WORK (& KNOWING WHY)
AGES 6–12, 160 PAGES, $12.95

GROWING UP READING

LEARNING TO READ THROUGH CREATIVE PLAY
AGES 1–6, 144 PAGES, $12.95

EARLY CHILDHOOD NEWS DIRECTORS' CHOICE AWARD
PARENTS' CHOICE APPROVED
PARENT'S GUIDE CHILDREN'S MEDIA AWARD

SCIENCE PLAY!

BEGINNING DISCOVERIES FOR 2- TO 6-YEAR-OLDS
AGES 2–6, 144 PAGES, $12.95

AMERICAN BOOKSELLER PICK OF THE LISTS
OPPENHEIM TOY PORTFOLIO BEST BOOK AWARD
TEACHER'S' CHOICE AWARD
BENJAMIN FRANKLIN BEST JUVENILE NONFICTION AWARD

SUPER SCIENCE CONCOCTIONS

50 MYSTERIOUS MIXTURES FOR FABULOUS FUN
AGES 6–12, 144 PAGES, $12.95

THE KIDS' NATURAL HISTORY BOOK
MAKING DINOS, FOSSILS, MAMMOTHS & MORE
BY JUDY PRESS

AMERICAN BOOKSELLER PICK OF THE LISTS
OPPENHEIM TOY PORTFOLIO BEST BOOK AWARD
BENJAMIN FRANKLIN BEST EDUCATION/TEACHING
  BOOK AWARD
THE KIDS' SCIENCE BOOK
CREATIVE EXPERIENCES FOR HANDS-ON FUN
BY ROBERT HIRSCHFELD &
NANCY WHITE

PARENTS' CHOICE GOLD AWARD
DR. TOY BEST VACATION PRODUCT
THE KIDS' NATURE BOOK
365 INDOOR/OUTDOOR ACTIVITIES
AND EXPERIENCES
BY SUSAN MILORD

AMERICAN BOOKSELLER PICK OF THE LISTS
OPPENHEIM TOY PORTFOLIO BEST BOOK AWARD
PARENTS' CHOICE APPROVED
PARENT'S GUIDE CHILDREN'S MEDIA AWARD
SUMMER FUN!
60 ACTIVITIES FOR A KID-PERFECT SUMMER
BY SUSAN WILLIAMSON

PARENTS' CHOICE APPROVED
PARENT'S GUIDE CHILDREN'S MEDIA AWARD
BOREDOM BUSTERS!
THE CURIOUS KIDS' ACTIVITY BOOK
BY AVERY HART AND PAUL MANTELL

PARENTS MAGAZINE PARENTS' PICK
KIDS LEARN AMERICA!
BRINGING GEOGRAPHY TO LIFE WITH PEOPLE,
PLACES, & HISTORY
BY PATRICIA GORDON & REED C. SNOW

CHILDREN'S BOOK-OF-THE-MONTH CLUB SELECTION
KIDS' COMPUTER CREATIONS
USING YOUR COMPUTER FOR ART & CRAFT FUN
BY CAROL SABBETH

VISIT OUR WEBSITE!
TO SEE WHAT'S NEW AT WILLIAMSON AND LEARN MORE ABOUT OTHER WILLIAMSON'S *KIDS CAN!®* BOOKS FOR AGES 5 TO 13, OUR *KALEIDOSCOPE KIDS®* BOOKS FOR AGES 7 TO 13, OUR *QUICK STARTS™ FOR KIDS!* BOOKS FOR AGES 7 AND OLDER, OR TO INQUIRE ABOUT SPECIFIC BOOKS, VISIT OUR WEBSITE AT:
www.williamsonbooks.com

TO ORDER BOOKS:
YOU'LL FIND WILLIAMSON BOOKS WHEREVER HIGH-QUALITY CHILDREN'S BOOKS ARE SOLD, OR ORDER DIRECTLY FROM WILLIAMSON PUBLISHING. WE ACCEPT VISA AND MASTERCARD (PLEASE INCLUDE THE NUMBER AND EXPIRATION DATE).

TOLL-FREE PHONE ORDERS WITH CREDIT CARDS:
1-800-234-8791

OR, SEND A CHECK WITH YOUR ORDER TO:

WILLIAMSON PUBLISHING COMPANY
P.O. BOX 185
CHARLOTTE, VERMONT 05445

E-MAIL ORDERS WITH CREDIT CARDS:
order@williamsonbooks.com
CATALOG REQUEST: MAIL, PHONE, OR E-MAIL

PLEASE ADD $3.20 FOR POSTAGE FOR ONE BOOK PLUS 50 CENTS FOR EACH ADDITIONAL BOOK. SATISFACTION IS GUARANTEED OR FULL REFUND WITHOUT QUESTIONS OR QUIBBLES.

PRICES MAY BE SLIGHTLY HIGHER WHEN PURCHASED IN CANADA.